Sculpting

MYTHICAL CREATURES

out of POLYMER CLAY

QUARRY

BEVERLY MASSACHUSETTS

Sculpting
MYTHICAL CREATURES
out of POLYMER CLAY

Make a Gnome, Pixie, Halfling, Fairy,
Mermaid, Gorgon, Vampire, Griffin,
Sphinx, Unicorn, Centaur,
Leviathan, and Dragon!

QUARRY BOOKS

DINKO and
BORIS TILOV

First published in the United States of America by
Quarry Books, a member of
Quarto Publishing Group USA Inc.
100 Cummings Center
Suite 406-L
Beverly, Massachusetts 01915-6101
Telephone: (978) 282-9590
Fax: (978) 283-2742
www.quarrybooks.com

Library of Congress Cataloging-in-Publication Data

Tilov, Dinko.
  Sculpting mythical creatures out of polymer clay : make a gnome, pixie, halfling, fairy, mermaid, gorgon, vampire, griffin, sphinx, unicorn, centaur, leviathan, and dragon! / Dinko and Boris Tilov.
     p. cm.
  ISBN-13: 978-1-59253-514-9
  ISBN-10: 1-59253-514-3
  1. Polymer clay craft. 2. Animals, Mythical, in art. I. Tilov, Boris. II. Title.
  TT297.T578 2009
  731.4'2—dc22

                                            2008039714

  ISBN-13: 978-1-59253-514-9
  ISBN-10: 1-59253-514-3

Design: Sandra Salamony
Photography: Dinko and Boris Tilov

Printed in USA

DEDICATION

To:

Irinka
Ivan
Maria
Sophia
Irina and Ustinian

CONTENTS

INTRODUCTION

This is a book about the creatures that live in myths: gnomes, fairies, nymphs, griffins, mermaids, centaurs, the sphinx, the leviathan, and unicorns. Throughout the history of art, a countless number of artists have tackled the representation of mythical characters and scenes based on episodes from Greek, Roman, Eastern, and Judeo-Christian myths. The mythical creatures—magical half men/half beasts—described in these stories have served as inspiration for a myriad of stone sculptures, oil paintings, and other contemporary works.

You, too, can take a peek into the mythical lands and see for yourself what these creatures look like. However, you do not need a heavy block of marble and a chisel, nor do you need years of training to invite mythical folk to cross over from their magical realms into our own. This book will teach you the mystical skills of a guide who can lead creatures through time and space, from imaginary universes to universes mundane. Here you will learn how to sculpt them out of polymer clay.

***

If you have the habit of looking at the last dozen of pages of a book before deciding whether you want it or not, you might notice that there are some rather complex-looking projects. Not to worry; we are pretty confident that everyone can roll a clay ball and make a long clay cylinder (referred to in this book as a snake). If you are capable of rolling a clay ball and making a snake, you have all the qualifications necessary to become the creator of your own mythical crowd.

The designs in this book are arranged so that you will hone your sculpting skills with each subsequent project, building on what you already know. You can get some serious results by following a series of easy-to-perform steps.

You will learn how to apply your newly acquired skills or brush up on basic sculpting skills using a great medium—polymer clay. Polymer clay is a versatile modeling material that is easy to work with. You do not need to buy expensive tools, make a big mess, or look for a huge work space. You can bake the finished sculptures in your home oven, like a tray of cookies.

In a nutshell:

What is it? A book on sculpting mythical creatures out of polymer clay.

Who it is for? Anyone.

What you can do with it? Make mythical and real creatures.

What you need to get started? This book, some clay, and mostly tools you already have around the house.

Why might you want to get started? To have some fun and get some ideas for projects or art classes.

Where can you go from here? With the skills we acquire and practice here, you can go anywhere your imagination leads you.

polymer clay
ESSENTIALS

Clay

Polymer clay is a plastic modeling compound that you can find at any arts and crafts store. It comes in different colors and can be baked in your home oven. The history of polymer clay as an art medium is only a few decades old. All brands of polymer clay contain a base of polyvinyl chloride (PVC), plasticizers, and pigments. It is called clay because the working properties and the texture resemble those of regular mineral clay. The leading polymer clay brands are Sculpey, Fimo, Cernit, Premo, Formello, and Kato clay. They each offer a wide range of colors and special-effect colors. Beads, jewels, small sculptures, figurines, and all kinds of boxes and vessels are some of the items commonly made from polymer clay. Polymer clay artists and amateurs call themselves clayers.

Tools

You do not need any sophisticated or expensive tools to shape the clay. Most of the suitable tools can be found around the house: pins, drill bits, needles, box cutters, wire, baking foil, pliers, manicure tools such as cuticle pushers, and scissors. Some enthusiasts prefer to also have on hand traditional sculptor's tools or a pasta machine to condition the clay. These items are easy to find at a reasonable price. Many polymer clay virtuosos make their own tools, too—just cover part of a regular nail and here is your first tool.

One common tool that we use consistently is a clay shaper. Clay shapers have a handle like a paintbrush and a rubber tip, which comes in a few different shapes. They are available in arts and crafts stores. The purpose of using clay shapers is to give you an option for a standardized

tool that you can obtain, because we do not expect you to have the same whatnots in your kitchen and garage drawers. But any tool can be replaced by another because there are many ways to do the same job. So if you don't have one, don't worry—just improvise. For a work surface you can use a ceramic tile, a plastic dining set, or glass.

Color and Size

The projects in this book do not prescribe a specific size for any of the creatures we show how to make. Everybody's hands and fingers are differently sized, so you should pick the size that is most comfortable for you to work with. As long as you keep the sizes of each body part proportional to the others, your creature will look great.

One of the most common questions about polymer clay projects is: "How much clay is needed for this project?" The best answer to this question is an old builder's proverb about the quantity of construction materials needed: It is not enough until there is leftover. The same goes for polymer clay.

As for colors, just make sure they match and you are all set. There is no reason why a purple mermaid should not have a pink fish tail and electric green hair. Always remember that you can mix new colors by using the ones you have; just as with paint, when you knead some yellow and blue clay together, you will get green clay.

Baking

Polymer clay stays soft until cured at a relatively low temperature 265° to 275°F (129° to 135°C), for 15 minutes per ¼" (6 mm) of thickness. The temperature needed for baking or curing of polymer clay is within the capabilities of every ordinary kitchen oven.

Various manufacturers give slightly different instructions for curing, most of which are in the above range. You should always bake your creations following the specific manufacturer's instructions on the package.

Polymer clay can be cured several times. Baked clay does not shrink or change shape and texture, so you can keep building with soft clay on top of already-baked elements.

Getting Started

If you are new to working with polymer clay, here are some recommendations: Always read and follow the instructions a particular manufacturer of polymer clay gives for their product. Don't start by buying huge quantities of clay and innumerable tools. What do you need if you are a complete novice? Not much. A few blocks of clay, any book about polymer clay, a pin, a ceramic tile for a work surface, and some baking foil. If by chance you do not end up hooked on playing with polymer clay for the rest of your life, there is always the comfort that you probably have spent less money than you would on a movie ticket.

What if you like it? Then the next things you need probably are a piece of artist's wire, small flat-nose pliers, small linemen's pliers, a taper-point clay shaper, and a cup-round clay shaper and some more clay. When you start a project, start with only one block of polymer clay of each color you will need, not more.

chapter 1

GNOMES

Rollieball Dropletson, the Gnome

This tiny gnome, with his pointy red hat, is the project that will teach anyone who is new to polymer clay or sculpting how to make and combine simple shapes to create a living creature from head to toe. We make everything out of tiny balls, snakes, and droplike shapes of clay.

You only need two ordinary tools—a work surface and a cutter—and two magical ones—your hands. The color scheme here is a recommendation. When choosing your colors make sure to pick vivid, well-contrasting colors.

Last but not least, make up a story to go along with your critter. No creature should be left without a story.

MATERIALS
• polymer clay in the following colors: brown, green, white, black, gray, purple, flesh, red

TOOLS
• cutter, ceramic tile

TIME FRAME
• 30 minutes (excluding baking time)

So hear all, hear all, about Rollieball:
Rollieball Dropletson is a gnome.
One of the finest specimens of the gnome genome.
His family tree takes a whole tome
in the "Who's Who" book of the race of gnomes.
One of his grandpas once went as far as Rome.
Why he is called Rollieball?
No one can recall.
There is a general suspicion though, that it is because
he looks as though he is made out of balls.
As for the family name, well,
this gnome appeared for the first time after an entire week of rainfall.

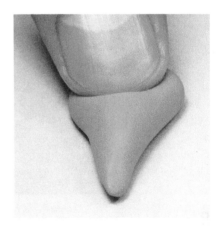

1. Roll a small (one-eighth of a 25g clay block) ball between the palms of your hands; if you have larger hands, roll between your index finger and thumb.

2. Squeeze one end of the ball and roll it between your thumb and middle finger. The goal is to end up with a raindrop-like shape, pointy at one end and round at the other. Make two raindrops as shown.

3. Put them at an approximate 90-degree angle to each other on your work surface. With your thumb, press the back part of the raindrops. These are the gnome's shoes. The two dents in the back of the shoes will host the rotund belly of the gnome.

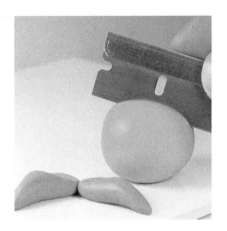

4. Roll a green ball of clay and cut it in half.

5. Roll a white ball of clay, the same size as the green ball, and cut it in half.

6. Put the two half-balls together to make a two-colored ball. Place that ball on the shoes with the white part of it on the top. The white part of the ball will be the gnome's shirt and the green part will be the gnome's pants or kilt, or whatever it is that gnomes wear these days.

7. Roll a flesh-colored ball of clay for the gnome's head. Generally this ball has to be smaller than the green and white ball. What happens if you make it the same size or bigger? You will just end up making a very smart gnome since there is going to be more space for brains in his head.

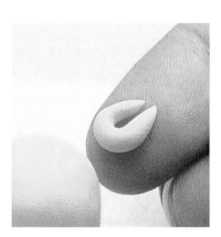

8. Next, roll a very small ball of flesh-colored clay to make an ear. If you are worried about proportions and wonder how small this ball must be, observe the ears of your friends, relatives, parents, or classmates. What is the size of their ears compared to their head? This is the correct proportion.

9. Roll the ball into a snake with two pointy ends. Do the same thing as in step 2 but this time do it on both sides of the ball.

10. Bend the snake from step 9 in the middle. Join the pointy ends. They must form one pointy end of the ear. The thick part will be the earlobe. Attach the ear to the head. Repeat this step twice, once for the left side of the head and once for the right side.

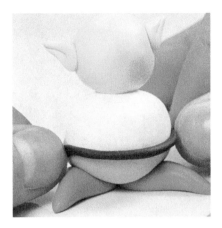

11. Here is a gnome in the making, all ears.

12. Roll a long, thin black snake. The length of the snake should be half of the gnome's belly circumference. This is the gnome's belt. We are making only half the belt since this is the only half that will be visible. The back part of the belt will be covered by the coat, so there is no need to make the other half.

MISCHIEVOUS COLORS

Some colors of polymer clay will stick to the hands. After using these, other color clays you touch will get dirty. These "sticky" colors vary among the different brands of clay, but generally are black, red, and green, in that order of intensity. You might need to wash your hands after handling the trousers of the gnome, to avoid soiling his sparkling white shirt.

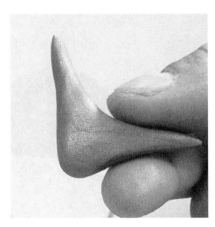

13. Make a gray, boomerang-like shape for the beard.

14. Bend the thin ends inward a little and attach the beard to the face as shown. Note that if you use colors with glitter or metallic effects, it might be a good idea to wash your hands once more. Depending on your goal, you may choose not to wash them. (If you were making a fairy, for example, it might be desirable to have it all covered in glitter, or "fairy dust," the substance that makes you fly.)

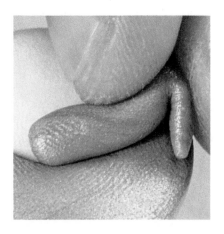

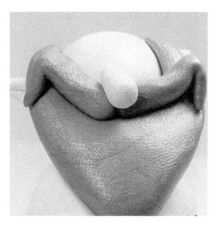

15. The next very important step is to add the moustache. In the gnome world, the saying goes, "A kiss without a moustache is as a meal without spice." So roll a tiny tapered shape between your fingers and attach it to the middle of the face, and in the middle of the beard. Be sure that the pointy ends point upward.

16. Put your index finger in the middle of the right part of the moustache and with your thumb bend it down. Push down slightly with your index finger to curve the moustache. This creates the gnome's smile. Repeat the last two steps, only this time make a mirror image for the other half of the moustache.

17. Make a flesh-colored droplet, big enough to be the gnome's nose, as shown in step 2. The lower end of the nose must cover the moustache. Attach the thin part of the droplet to the head.

18. Roll two small white balls for the eyes. Attach them on both sides of the nose.

19. Here the gnome starts to take shape. Now it is time to give him style. Choose a cool, vibrant color for his overcoat. In this case our choice is blue. Make a ball about as big as the head.

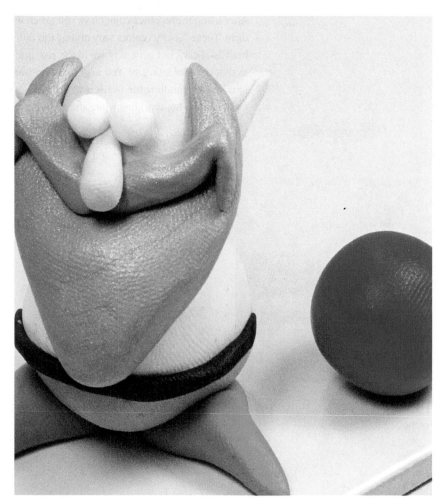

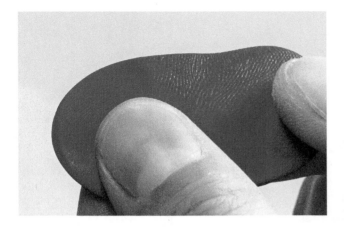

20. Flatten the ball between your index fingers and thumbs to make an elliptical, flat piece of clay. This is the gnome's coat.

21. Turn the work surface around and help the gnome put on his coat. The coat must cover half the head and about three-quarters of the body length and width. Make sure that the coat covers the belt both from the left and the right sides.

22. Place your thumb and index finger on the left and right side of the gnome, exactly between the body ball and the head. Squeeze gently.

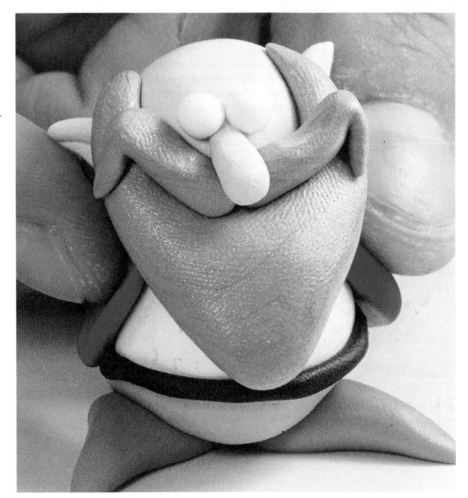

23. At this point you might wonder why a small crowd of critters has gathered around your work surface. Who are they? What do they want? Not to worry. These are other gnomes; they can sense when a new gnome is being created and, of course, they are curious by nature. They want to make the new gnome on the block feel welcome.

24. Make two roughly cylindrical shapes from the same color that you used for the coat.

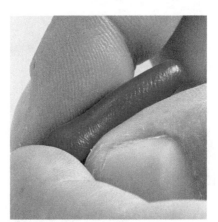
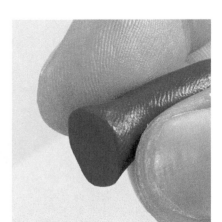

25. Flatten the larger end of the cylinder. Make a small dent at that end. This is the sleeve of the coat.

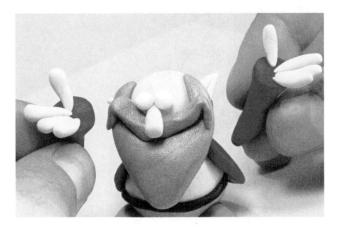

26. Make eight flesh-colored longish raindrops for the fingers.

27. Attach them to the sleeve. Why only eight fingers? There are basically two schools of gnome anatomy: the lazy school and the laborious academy. The laborious academy supports the theory that gnome anatomy is close if not identical to the human anatomy, and hence, dwarves have ten fingers. If you choose to uphold this point of view, please feel free to make ten fingers. The lazy school, on the other hand, claims that four fingers on a hand look exactly the same as five fingers, since no one ever really counts.

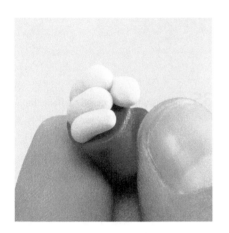

28. Bend the fingers into a fist.

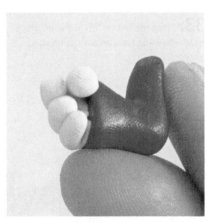

29. Bend the arm between your index finger and thumb to form an elbow.

30. Attach the arm to the body.

31. Repeat the last two steps for the other arm. Be sure to make a mirror image. There is no need to end up with two left hands or two right hands. The thumbs define left and right for the hands; observe your own hands as a reference. Place the thumb at a right angle to his index and other fingers.

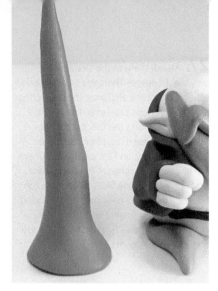

32. The hat of the gnome should be at least as tall as the critter. Make it the same way you made the sleeves; the only difference is that the hat is pointy.

33. Place the hat on top of the gnome's head. Now you have an almost finished gnome.

35. Here is your first creature. Bake the finished character according to the clay manufacturer's instructions.

34. Attach two short gray snakes to the head, close to the eyes, for the eyebrows. Roll two minuscule balls of black clay and place them in the middle of the eyeballs. This is the step that brings the creature to life.

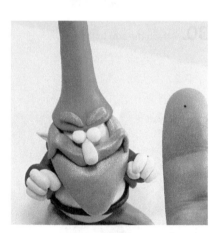

Sculpting Mythical Creatures out of Polymer Clay

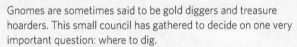

variations

Gnomes are sometimes said to be gold diggers and treasure hoarders. This small council has gathered to decide on one very important question: where to dig.

This is an easy trick to create different gnome characters. Take a ball for the head, attach the nose, eyes, and ears, and scratch a smile. Here is your first gnome character: the bald gnome. Add a moustache and curve the ends of the moustache, and here is a hussar soldier character (the second one from the left). Make a wide curved-down mustache and here is one of the passengers in the nutshell boat. Make a thin moustache and curve it downward, and here is your sheriff character. Add a long beard and here is your druid priest. Generally, adding different facial hair to the same head produces a huge variety of characters quite easily.

Create an even simpler version of a gnome, where the mouth is drawn straight on a ball of clay on which the eyes, nose, and ears are stuck.

Rollieball is not the only one who sprung up after a week of rainfall—mushrooms tend to do that, too. Mushrooms are also the preferred accommodation for gnomes—they make very cozy homes and are just the right size for one gnome.

chapter 2
PIXIES

Brice, the Pixie

MATERIALS
- polymer clay in the following colors: blue, pink/purple, glow-in-the-dark
- wire

TOOLS
- cutter
- taper-point clay shaper
- cup-round clay shaper
- pliers
- wire cutters

TIME FRAME
- 30 to 60 minutes (excluding baking time)

Forest-dwelling creatures are all related. The quick-witted pixies, who we meet here, are cousins of the elves, who are cousins of the imps, who are in turn distant cousins of the garden dwarves, some of whom we ran into just a project ago.

The quick-witted, nimble-fingered, bristly-red-haired pixies belong to the more mischievous part of this big extended family. They particularly enjoy the company of black sheep. Whenever these pixies stray into the woods, they can be found easily, picking berries right under the nose of other forest critters. Pixies turn purple when they blush and navy blue when they play out in the sun for too long.

While making a pixie, you will learn how to create slightly more complicated shapes than those of the gnome. We will practice making a more humanlike face. We will, for the first time, use a bit of armature, to introduce the concept.

This pixie's name is Brice,
we will not repeat it twice.
For his head there is a price.
And to tell you the truth it is fair and nice—
it is a goblet of gold, we are told,
and it doesn't matter if you catch him now or
    when he is old.
Brice comes from a famous clan of the Bluedan.
Brice hid the English general's horse without
    any remorse.

He stole and drank his best whiskey
and what about the mood of the General Husky.
The General is very sad and really, really mad.
And the story's twist would have been really bad
if it weren't for the fact that Brice knew how to act,
and not to get sacked,
because he is a blue pixie, a proverbial trickster
and a proud descendant of wild highlanders.

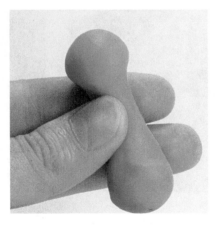

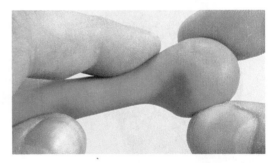

1. Roll a ball or an egglike shape between the palms of your hands.

2. Hold the egglike shape and roll between your thumb and index and middle fingers as shown. You should end up with a dumbbell shape. One of the round ends will be the pixie's body and the other one, his head.

3. Hold as shown and slightly tilt to one side the part you chose for a head. You can choose which end is the head and which is the bottom without giving it too much thought; pixie scholars will tell you that the difference is really quite small.

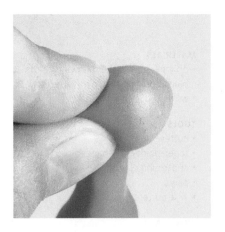

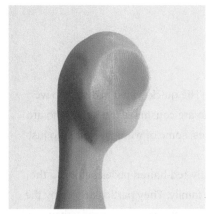

4. To make a nose, squeeze between your index finger and thumb the part of the head that sticks out. Make sure not to grab too much clay between your fingertips, because pixies have narrow noses. You can see the dent left by your fingertip.

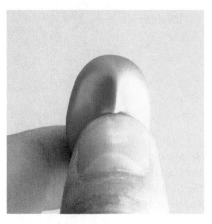

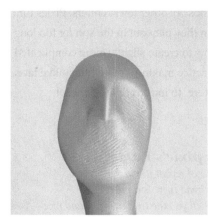

5. Now turn around the prospective pixie to face you and as shown push with your thumb to define the length of the nose. Hold the back of the critter's head in the process.

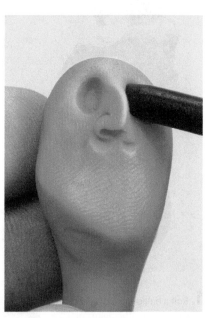

6. Using the handle tip of the cup-round clay shaper, define the outer nostrils of the pixie as shown. Give the creature large nostrils to enable him to smell trouble from afar.

7. Using the taper-point clay shaper, poke two holes for the inner nostrils; make sure to push in a direction opposite to the outer nostril, and not toward the inside of the head. That way the nostrils you defined on the outside will flare up slightly; they will have volume on the outside and be hollow on the inside.

8. Use the handle tip of the clay shaper to poke two eye sockets.

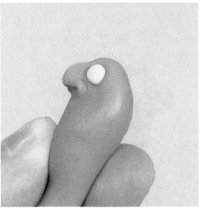

9. Fill these to the brim with two balls of glow-in-the-dark clay. This is the color of choice for the eyes and bones of all the creatures that we make in this book.

10. By now you have probably noticed that our pixie has the strong jaw of a thug. That is something to be remedied, because mischievous as they may be, pixies are rather skinny critters. Roll between your index finger and thumb to get rid of any excessive jaw.

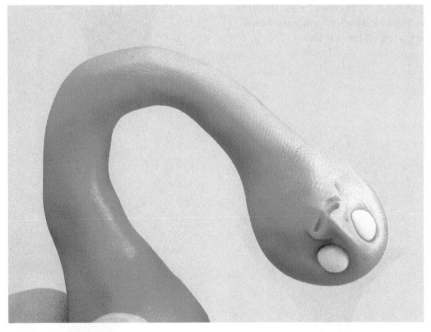

11. Our pixie is starting to have a thin long neck, as it should. Note that at a later stage we will put a bit of wire inside the neck to support it. For now, the long neck and the body also serve as a handle to hold the creature while you work on his head.

12. It looks like we are pulling the pixie's ear, doesn't it? Gently pinch the sides of the head, at the level of the nose, to extract two ears out of the bulk of the head. The result is a ridge, much like the one we obtained when making the nose.

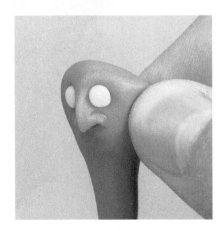

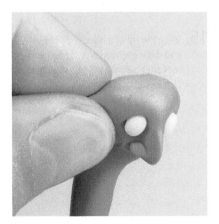

13. Use a cutter or a fingernail to define the ear from the top. The pixie's earlobe will not be separated but will be glued to the head. Pull on the ear some more. With your index finger and thumb, gently squeeze the tip of the ear to make it pointier. When in doubt with mythical creatures, make the ears pointy. At this point the ear should be quite thin and two-dimensional, which is important for the next step.

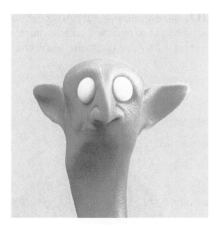

14. Fold the edges of the ear inward as shown. Put a small hole in the ear using a clay shaper.

15. With the tip of a needle, poke two holes and draw eyebrows as shown. You can later (after baking) insert two specks of black clay inside these holes.

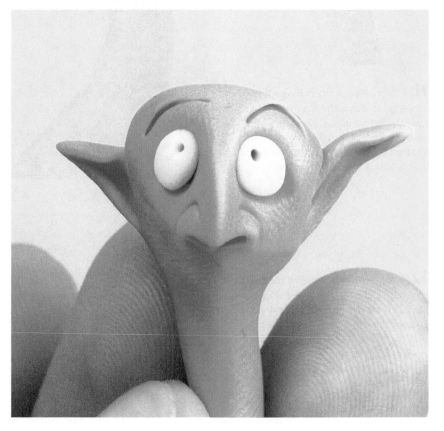

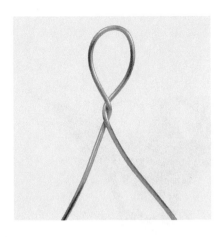

16. As we saw earlier, the thin neck of the pixie is too easy to bend. This is why we will insert a bit of wire to enable the critter to stand upright. This is the basic building block of armature building, which will be used quite frequently throughout this book to be able to make delicate characters with thin parts and long limbs. For better or worse, not all mythical folk are merry chubsters, as we may have led you to think with the gnome. Bend a piece of wire in two and start twisting the two ends around each other as shown. You should end up with one loopy end, sometimes called "the spoon," and one bristly end sometimes called "the fork."

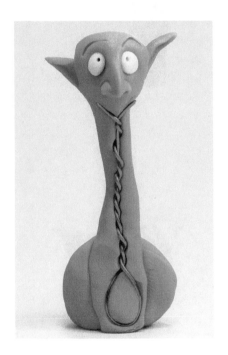

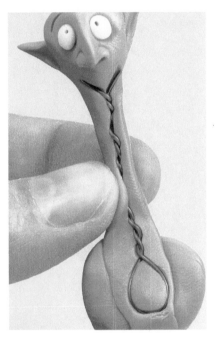

17. Insert the armature in the neck and body of the creature and gently push it in. Notice that we had to add some more clay to the torso.

18. Gently cover the wire with the surrounding clay. You can later smudge with your fingers and a clay shaper to eliminate the seams.

19. Push the head down and forward. The Y-shaped end of the armature (the fork) digs deeper into the head, and in the process the creature's mouth is defined.

20. Using your fingers and a clay shaper, eliminate the seams that are left over after covering up the wire with clay.

21. Use a small, irregularly shaped bit of glow-in-the-dark-clay to make a tooth. The choice of number of teeth is entirely yours. Just remember that pixies are not sharks, if you feel you are starting to get carried away.

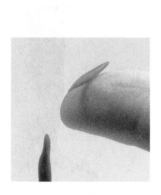

22. We will now proceed to give the pixie a fashionable haircut—hair by hair. Individual hairs are made by rolling small balls of purple clay between your fingertips until you get tiny snakes with two pointy ends. You can stick these to the pixie's head either one by one, or make a tuft first and then place it on top of the pixie's head. A mohawk-like hairstyle is not uncommon among the pixies of this world. Do not forget to give your pixie sideburns as well. When you stick the sideburns to the face, the first point of contact should be the middle of each individual hair, as this is the thickest part; then you can leave the lower end hanging while the upper one blends in the hair.

23. Roll a blue snake, fold it in two, and stick it to the face as shown to make a lower lip. Make sure to leave some distance between the lower lip and the central teeth.

24. Now that we have a head, neck, and torso, it is high time we gave the pixie arms and legs. Make a paw by squishing a ball of clay between your index finger and thumb into a disk. Note, however, that one end of the disk should be thin while the other one remains round; the thin end will be attached to the body of the pixie, while the round end will serve as toes.

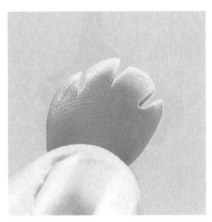

25. Using a cutter, divide the fatter part of the paw into several toes as shown.

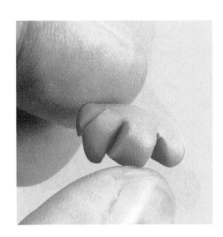

26. Using a cutter gives each individual toe sharp edges. To fix this, gently spread all the toes out and touch the edges of each toe with the tip of your finger.

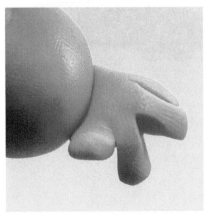

27. Firmly stick the thin part of the toe to the bottom of the critter.

28. Spread out the toes and make the big toe stick out.

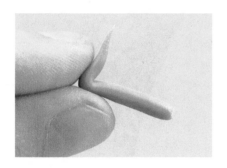

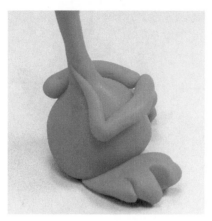

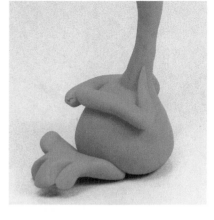

29. We next turn to the arms. Make a snake with one pointy and one round end and bend it at a right angle as shown.

30. Attach the arms to the body with the pointy end at shoulder height and the round parts almost crossed on the belly.

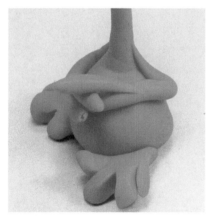

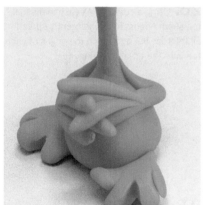

31. Make several snakes, just like the one for the arm, only slightly smaller. Stick them on top of each other, as shown, with the pointy ends attached at the wrist of the pixie. Note that the snake we use for the pinkie is shorter than the one used for the middle finger, which is in turn shorter than the one used for the index finger.

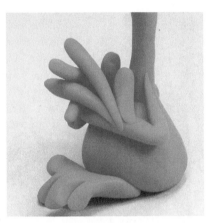

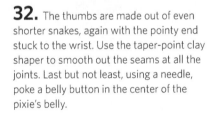

32. The thumbs are made out of even shorter snakes, again with the pointy end stuck to the wrist. Use the taper-point clay shaper to smooth out the seams at all the joints. Last but not least, using a needle, poke a belly button in the center of the pixie's belly.

33. Here is your pixie; his hands are itching for action! Bake the finished character according to the clay manufacturer's instructions.

variations

Pixies are flocking together, something's going on . . . .

chapter 3

HALFLINGS

Mr. Gladden, the Halfling

Halflings are twice as short as a grown-up person, hence their name. Although not giants in posture, halflings have large souls and are kind and welcoming to anyone who doesn't look down on them. They like to walk barefoot in the lush meadows. They brew and drink foamy ales until their ears get slightly pointier than usual in the process and begin to tingle. Hop bits can often be found all over their hilly dwellings and cottages. Halflings are merry folk who are quite energetic and lighthearted.

In this project you will learn how to make a good-natured, humanlike creature standing on two legs. To do this we will take armature making one step further. You will also practice making clothes and experimenting with hairstyles. We will also come one step closer to making a human face.

MATERIALS
- polymer clay in the following colors: green, orange, flesh, brown, yellow, glow-in-the-dark
- wire

TOOLS
- taper-point clay shaper
- cup-round clay shaper
- cutter
- needle
- pliers
- wire cutters

TIME FRAME
- 60 to 90 minutes (excluding baking time)

Blink, blink—

here appears Mr. Gladden the halfling.
If you see him, wink in assent.
And please, wink again in assent
if you feel around him the good scent.
It is the magic smell, the halfling's spell
of homemade cookies with which the lunch ends well.
Do you see how his smile foretells
a quiet afternoon with quiet doorbells,
rather longish naps
or storytelling with friendly chaps?

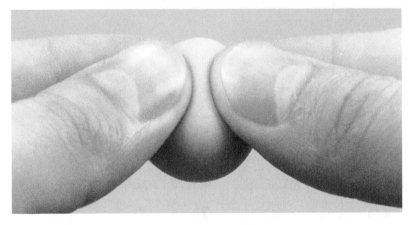

1. We start by making the halfling's face and head. The series of steps we perform here are almost the same as the ones we used to make the pixie's face. Here, though, we go for a rounder face. Roll a ball between the palms of your hands. This ball is the halfling's head.

2. Holding the back of the head with your index fingers, press with your thumbs as shown. Make sure to leave enough clay between your thumbs because this is the protrusion that we will use for the halfling's nose—and it has to be a big one. For the pixie we squeezed with the index finger and thumb so as to leave very little volume; here we use thumbs to make a bulkier nose.

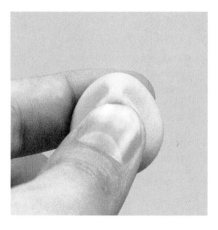

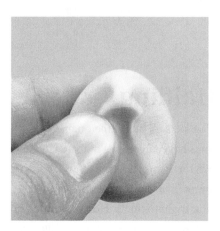

3. Push in as shown and slightly up using your thumb.

4. We will use the distortion in the clay to form the nostrils. Push on both sides of the nose. Push the whole nose slightly down and you will see the nostrils shape up.

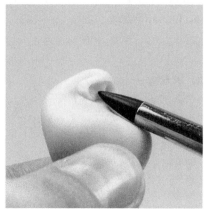

5. Use the taper-point and cup-round clay shapers to finish the nose, much in the same way we did for the pixie.

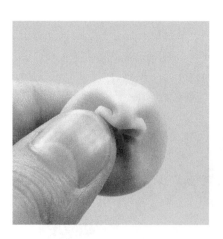

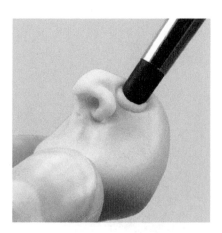

6. Finally, push up on the outer part of each nostril to flare them up a little.

7. Next, we do the eyes. Using the cup-round clay shaper, make an imprint on the clay above the nostril as shown.

8. Make a second push as shown just above the first one. The goal is to make a bag under the future eye. The eye itself is made by wrapping a ball of clay in a flat piece of clay—a squished short snake. This wrap is the eyelid. It should cover the upper part of the eye.

9. Stick the eyes to the head and use the tip of a needle to poke two deep holes for the eyes. Use the needle again to draw/cut out a smiling mouth in the halfling's face.

10. To make the cheeks of the smiling halfling, roll out a droplike shape that is very thick at one end but pointy at the other. Bend the shape in two. Attach it at the corner of the mouth and, using a clay shaper, smudge the pointy ends into the bulk of the face.

11. To make a lower lip, we roll out a snake that is round in the middle and pointy at the ends. Attach the thick middle part to the jaw and, using your fingers and a taper-point clay shaper, blend the pointy ends into the face.

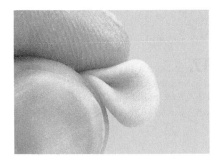

12. To make an ear, roll out a ball, then squish it into a disk between your fingers. As we did for the foot of the pixie, make one end of the disk thin and leave the other one thick. Fold the thin end as shown.

13. Attach the ears to the back of the head, at the level of the nose. Give the halfling a tiny button chin. With this step we have a head of sorts, so we can leave it aside for a little bit and work on something to put it on.

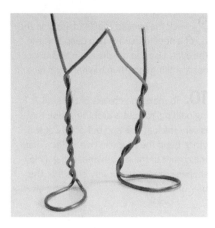

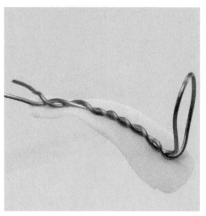

14. To make the legs of the halfling, we use the same armature shape as in the previous project. This time, however, we bend the loop at a right angle to the twisted part of the wire. A good test for the armature is whether it can stand alone.

15. Next, we put some flesh on the wire leg. Start covering with sheets of clay as shown. Once you have covered the whole leg, check again if it can stand upright on it own. If not, bend it a little forward vis-à-vis the foot. You can always give the halfling a bigger heel. Generally, the halflings that have the balance are the flat-footed ones.

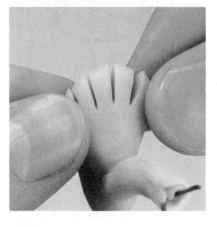

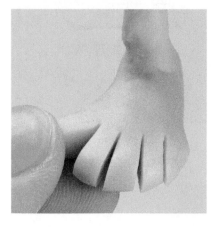

16. Using the same technique as you did on the pixie, cut out several toes in the foot of the halfling. The big toe should be almost twice as wide as the rest. Spread out the toes a little and round all the edges by touching them with the tip of your finger. It is a good thing we have not yet attached the legs to the halfling because halflings are a little ticklish. This, in part, explains why they are always smiling.

17. Squeeze with your fingers as shown to make a knee. You can also put a small disk of clay on top of the knee as a kneecap. (This is what we did for the chin of the halfling.)

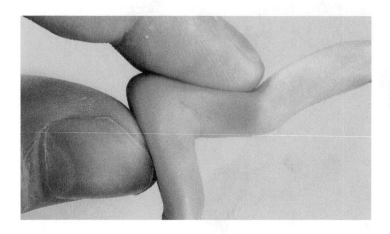

18. Bend the leg at the knee a little. This bending concerns the clay around the wire; the wire inside is still straight. In other words, it does not matter what the skeleton/armature looks like, as long as there is enough meat on the bones (clay on the wire).

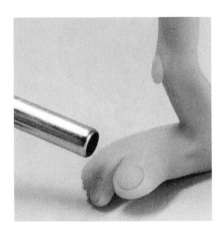

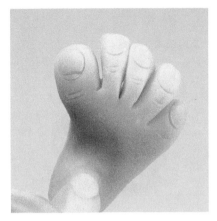

19. And now it is pedicure time! Use a small tube to leave round marks at the upper end of the toes—these are toenails. With a needle draw several horizontal lines in the middle of each toe. We skip the nail polish for now.

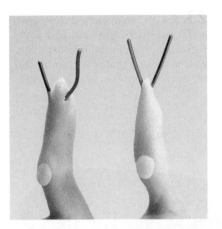

20. Here is a last look at the legs before we put them in the oven. We will bake the legs to make them strong enough to support the torso of the halfling, which is no easy task. Notice that at the upper end two bits of wire are still protruding from the clay coat and that the clay is somewhat tapered; in that way it will be easier to stick the hard-baked legs in the soft bottom of the halfling.

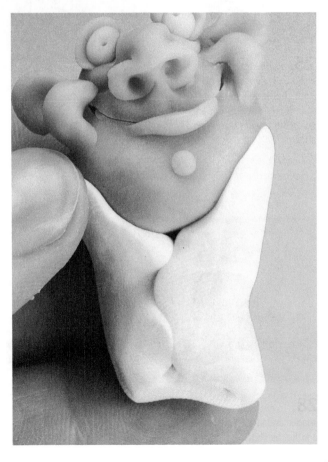

21. Halflings like to dress up. To create a tailor-made shirt, squish a ball of white clay flat to approximately the size and shape shown in the picture, and relative to the head. Proceed to wrap it around the lower part of the head and leave enough hanging for a torso.

22. Roll out a ball of brown clay, cut it in half, and stick the shirt-wearing halfling head on top of it as demonstrated.

23. Roll out two snakes and squish them flat for suspenders. These may cross at the back, although in this particular design we give the halfling a coat so you cannot really see that.

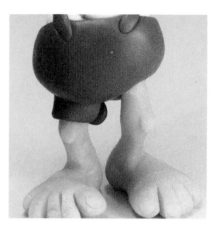

24. Make a pants leg by rolling out a short, fat snake, squishing it flat, and wrapping it around the leg and above the knee. Make sure that the upper part of the pants leg touches the bottom of the pants all around; otherwise, the pants look torn.

25. To make a coat, roll out a ball from a color of your choice and squish it flat, starting from the center and going out toward the edges as shown.

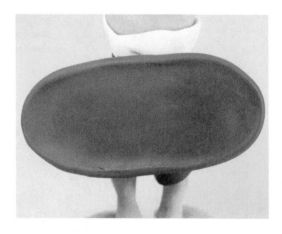

26. Gently pull on the disk you made in the previous step, to make an elliptical shape. Do not flatten all the way out the edge, leaving a small fringe all around the ellipse.

27. Now wrap the coat you just made around the halfling as shown. Make sure not to cover the suspenders. If this coat does not fit, make a shorter or longer one until you get it right.

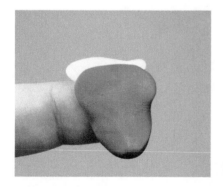

28. To make sleeves, make two flat shapes and stick them on top of one another as shown.

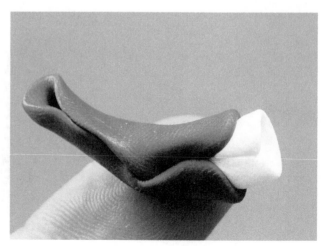

29. Next roll them in, as shown, keeping the white cuffs on the inside.

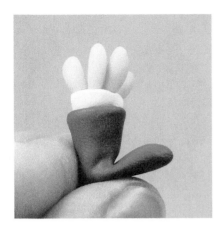

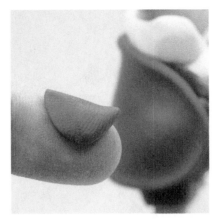

30. Roll out a couple of fingers, as we did for the gnome, and stick them to the inside of the sleeve. Bend the arm at the elbow.

31. Make a flat semicircle and attach it to the side of the coat with the help of a taper-point clay shaper. Do not stick the straight edge to the coat; this is the halfling's deep pocket.

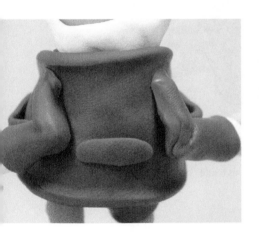

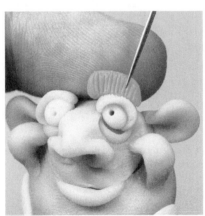

32. Turn the critter around and put a short belt on the back of the coat. Now is also the time to attach the arms to the body by firmly sticking the upper arm to the torso and using a clay shaper to smudge in at the shoulders.

33. Now that the halfling is all dressed and on his feet, we need to give some attention to his hair and facial hair. To make an eyebrow, put a short, thick worm on top of the eyelid. Using a needle, draw a number of adjacent lines, pulling from the eyelid up, while holding the back of the eyebrow.

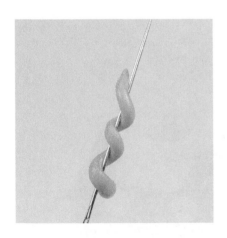

34. To make a hair coil, roll out a snake and twist it around the needle as shown, without squeezing it too much. Next, pull straight up to release the coil from the needle.

35. Stick the coil to the bald halfling's head.

36. Repeat the last two steps as many times as you wish until the halfling starts looking like the lion that he is.

37. Gently pinch the tips of the ears.

38. Make buttons out of small disks of clay. Push in the center of the disk with the tip of the clay shaper's handle.

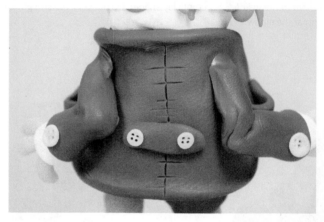

39. Using a needle put four holes in each button; draw a fly on the pants and seams (in the form of dotted lines) on the coat, pockets, and elsewhere. The right tool for the right job they say—it is only fitting that this haute couture work should be done with a needle.

40. Here is your halfling, ready to go about his highly important business. Bake the finished character according to the clay manufacturer's instructions.

variations

The more, the merrier.

Halflings have gathered around to convince the grumpy halfling to go for a walk with them.

Just when they had him convinced, the shy halfling disappears. Go figure!

chapter 4
FAIRIES

Gwen, the Fairy

Fairies are the fairest of the forest folk. These delicate beings have butterfly wings and play hide-and-seek with the rays of the sun in the crowns of the trees and play tag with the bees around the flower blossoms. That is in their spare time, when they are not busy helping birds with aching wings, fluffy rabbits stuck at the narrow entrances of their homes, slow turtles crossing the street, prickly hedgehogs trying to inflate a balloon for their young, penniless mice trying to buy ice cream, and all kinds of other tiny beasts in sizeable distress. Fairies try to make things happen for everyone, and yet find they the time to take care of their appearance.

In this project we make a full-body female human character. We learn to make wings using a technique derived from millefiori, one similar to that which is employed while cutting salami and similar meats, as the pepperoni pizza eaters among you will recognize. We practice intricate clothing and body details and elaborate hairstyles.

MATERIALS
- polymer clay in the following colors: flesh, glow-in-the-dark, silver, gold, black, dark green

TOOLS
- cutter
- taper-point clay shaper
- cup-round clay shaper
- needle
- roller/tube

TIME FRAME
- 60 to 120 minutes (excluding baking time)

If you leave your window open
on a moon-lit summer night,
the fairies will fly into your room.
They will mend all the things that make
    you worry.
They will show you strange fairy gimmicks
and introduce you to a friendly phoenix.
So use your imagination, don't leave it
    on standby,
it is something that you must apply

and if you see something that is small and bright
in the middle of the night
it may not be a firefly.
Look carefully,
and even if it tries to hide behind a bonsai
and is really shy, go and say hi.
It may be that a fairy stopped by,
that has a story to tell
and make a spell
before it bids you farewell.

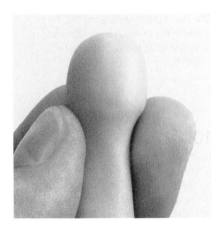

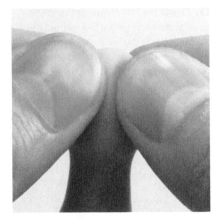

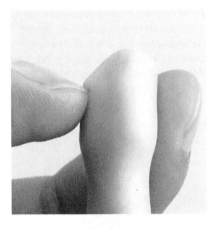

1. Start by making a basic shape like the one in the picture. It should roughly resemble a bowling pin. The head of the pin will be the fairy's head.

2. Very gently push with your thumbs on the upper part of the pin's head. Essentially this step is the same one that we performed to make the nose of the halfling, only here do not exert much pressure. Our goal is to make a small delicate nose, not a big fleshy one.

3. Push with a fingernail to set your preferred fairy nose length. Again, do not use much force; you only need to have a small line appear on the clay. The nose need not protrude much from the face. (Because if it did, you would have the lying Pinocchio.)

4. Make two shallow holes for the eyes using a taper-point clay shaper as shown.

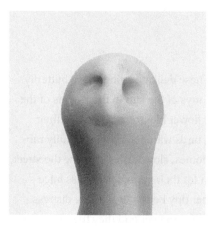

5. With your fingers, thin out the cheeks of the fairy little by little. You can either roll between index finger and thumb until you get the desired effect, or just push the clay in.

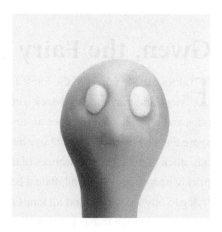

6. Insert two slightly squished balls in the eye sockets.

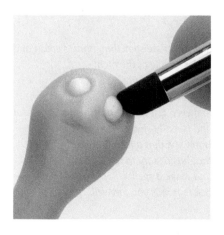

7. Using the cup-round clay shaper, touch all the outside contact points between the eyeball and the face. The goal of this exercise is to take away some of the roundness of the eyeball. Fairies are supposed to be pretty, so bulging eyes are to be avoided.

8. One of the facial features that distinguished the more gentle beings from the sturdier ones is the lower jaw. In this step we use a cutter to delimit the lower jaw of the fairy and separate it from the neck.

9. Touch the sharp edge of the jaw produced in the previous step with your fingers to soften it. Do the same to the neck.

10. Use a clay shaper to eliminate the traces from the surgery two steps ago. Note that while the warmth of your fingers softens the clay and helps smooth the larger surfaces, the clay shaper is used to do the finer detail and eliminate the smaller imperfections.

11. Using the tip of a needle, draw a mouth and eyebrows and poke four holes—two for the eyes and two for the nostrils. A small mouth is another defining feature of the delicate and dainty look we are after in this project.

Sculpting Mythical Creatures out of Polymer Clay

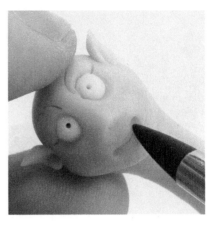

12. Make two droplike bits for ears.

13. Attach them firmly to the head by pressing with the taper-point clay shaper as shown.

14. Use the clay shaper to shape the corners of the mouth; gently rotate the tip of the clay shaper back and forth by pressing at the end of the mouth line you drew with the needle.

15. The nose of the fairy should point in the same direction as her ears—up. Gently push the nose up to make it chipped.

16. To make a lower lip for the fairy, roll out a minuscule snake and attach it just under the mouth line.

17. Smudge in all the ends of the lower lip into the chin except the upper side.

18. To finish the eyebrows, roll out two longish drops of hair-colored clay (you determine the color of the hair). Attach them to the forehead by the round part first—you can push with your finger there, while handling the pointy end with a clay shaper.

19. Next, to create the volume of the hair, put a lump of hair-colored clay on top of the fairy's head and wrap it around the head as a hat.

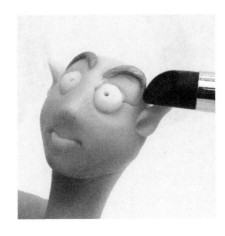

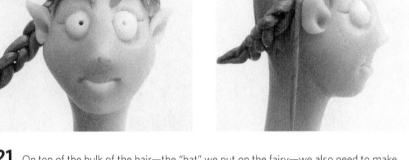

20. Use the clay shaper to thin out the hair around the temples.

21. On top of the bulk of the hair—the "hat" we put on the fairy—we also need to make individual hairs, streaks of hair, and create the impression of an elaborate hairstyle. Fairies like braiding each other's hair, so that has to show. For a crash or refresh course on braiding hair, refer to this series of photographs and the next step.

22. Begin by rolling out three long snakes of the same length. Stick their thicker ends firmly on the top of one another and to your work surface; only the juncture point between the three streaks of hair should stick to the work surface; we need to be able to move the rest of them around. Cross the right snake over the center one, and the left on top of the right one; they have effectively change places, but here we call them with their old names—the right one is the one that was on the right side in the first step. Next, place the original left one under the center one; then proceed to put the original right one under the original left one and on top of the center streak. Repeat this sequence of steps several times to make a full braid.

23. Here is the finished hairstyle. For the bun, make a thicker braid and roll it into an eddy.

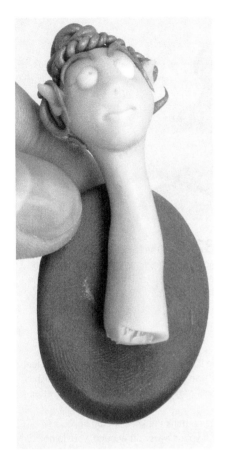

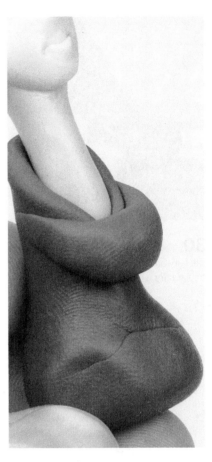

24. Squeeze a ball into an ellipse and place the fairy's neck on it. This will be the garment of the fairy, so pick your colors wisely. Generally earthy colors and glittery, metallic effects work best. Notice that we had to cut the neck to shorten it.

25. Wrap the ellipse around the neck to create the torso as shown. Leave a high collar at the back of the fairy's neck. Make sure that the fairy has a thin waist.

26. Roll out a snake and stick it to the chest as shown. Use a clay shaper to blend the edges at shoulder height.

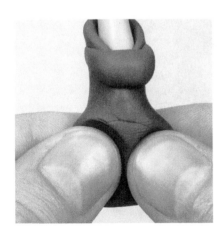

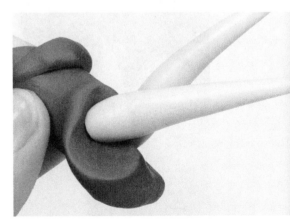

27. Using your index fingers and thumbs, hold with both hands and squeeze to produce the dress of the fairy.

28. Make two sockets in the dress with the help of the taper-point clay shaper.

29. Roll out two flesh-colored snakes, tapering toward one end and round at the other. These will be the fairy's legs. Insert the round end into the socket.

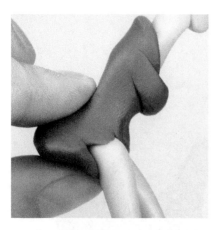 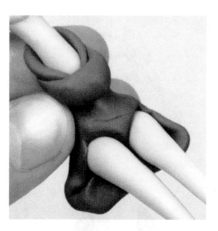 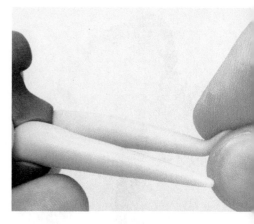

30. Fold the dress under the bottom of the fairy and squeeze as shown. This particular fairy will be sitting down.

31. Here is another look at the position of the legs with the dress wrapped around them. Do not cross the legs of the fairy yet because we still need to work on each leg individually to make the feet.

32. Hold the fairy by the waist. Using your index finger and thumb, squeeze the end of the leg to flatten it. This will be the foot of the fairy.

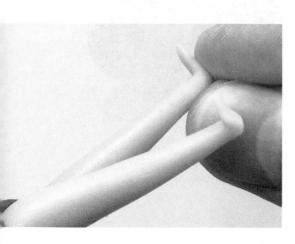

33. Gently bend the flattened bit at a right angle to the leg. Make sure that the fairy's feet are small, as this is another characteristic trait of these magical creatures that distinguishes them from the halflings with their giant feet. The less a fairy looks like a halfling, the better.

34. Cut out a small dent in the leg under where you think the knee should be. Use a taper-point clay shaper to smooth any roughness. If your clay is soft enough, you do not need to use a cutter to make the dent; you can push gently with your fingers or the handle of the clay shaper.

35. You can now cross the legs on top of each other. Notice that so far we used no armature to make a rather fragile-looking being; therefore, we need to make sure that the posture is such that the limbs are close to one another to minimize the danger of their accidentally breaking off.

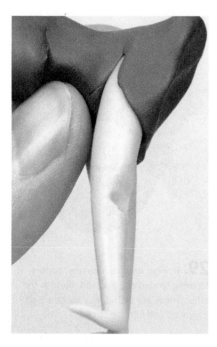 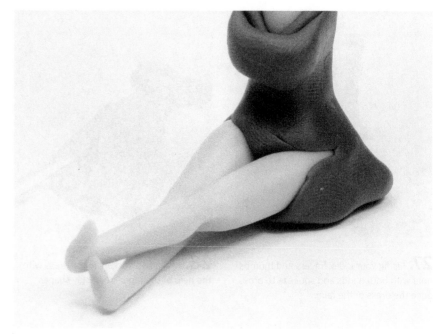

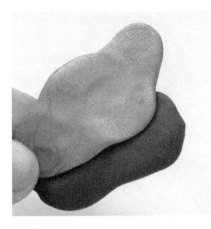

36. To make the details of the dress, we will use a technique loosely based on the popular polymer clay technique of millefiori. While in millefiori you would typically arrange different-colored clays in a carefully determined order, to obtain a certain effect with their cross-section, here we simply pick two well-contrasting colors and mix them up several times in a random order. Start with two flat overlapped pieces of clay as shown.

37. Twist them around each other and roll them into a ball.

38. Pinch one end of the ball as shown.

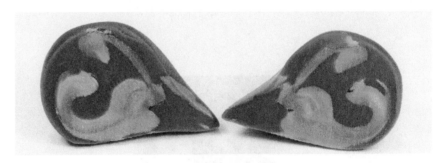

39. When you cut the lopsided, squished ball in two equal halves, your result should look something like this. Bear in mind that each cut produces two identical patterns. It is almost certain that yours will not look like the ones in the picture, simply because these are randomly generated by twisting and kneading the clay. If you are displeased with the first cut, cut out a second slice; look on both sides of the cutter—again you have two identical patterns.

40. After deciding which randomly generated pattern to use, cut out two slices and stick them on top of the fairy's thigh to embellish the plain forest green dress that she has been wearing so far.

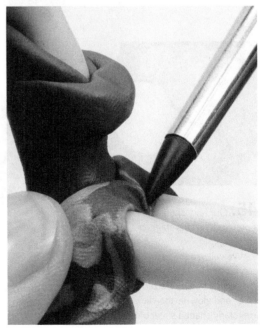

41. To make the arm of the fairy, roll out a snake and bend it at the elbow; the fatter end will be used to make the hand of the fairy. Squish that end flat, but do not quite make it two-dimensional.

42. Use a cutter to cut out several fingers as shown. The procedure is analogous to the one we used for the halfling's toes. The cut that separates the thumb should be a little farther in the general direction of the elbow.

43. Spread the fingers wide apart and with your fingertips touch them one by one to round them off. The rule for the length of the fingers is this: the middle finger is longest, the index finger a notch shorter, and the pinkie shortest. The thumb is slightly thicker and shorter than the rest—simply fold the designated thumb in two. The fingers of the fairy should be pointy, unlike the hot dog–like fingers of the majority of critters so far.

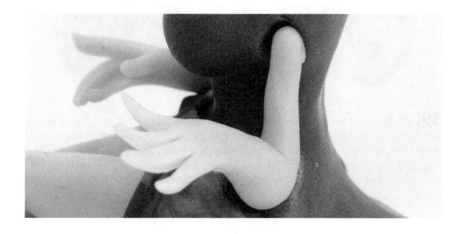

44. Make a small socket at the height of the fairy's shoulder. Attach the arm to the body at the elbow, with the upper arm running alongside the body, and place the top part in the socket.

45. Our fairy should be looking like a pretty girl at this stage, but she needs her wings.

We will use the same technique that we previously practiced to decorate the dress. Put several different-sized balls of gold, silver, and glow-in-the-dark clay on a flat, irregularly shaped sheet of black clay.

46. Wrap the sheet of black clay around them, knead once or twice and roll the whole thing into a ball.

47. Cut this peculiar fruit in four pieces, just like you would cut an orange or an apple.

48. Put the fruit back together, only this time stick the peels to the inside as shown. Although we rely on the forces of nature to produce the pattern of the wings, direct the process by choosing well-contrasting colors and arrange them to avoid a concentration of too much black.

49. Roll the whole thing into a ball. You can knead it once or twice prior to that if you wish. The more you knead, the smaller the sections of color and the less contrasting the pattern will be.

50. Cut out several slices of the strange fruit until you get two pairs of patterns you like for the wings.

51. Use a small tube or a roller to flatten the slices. This helps to make the metallic clay shine because glittering metal bits get packed closer together.

52. Stick the four slices on top of each other as shown. Notice that the slices are not exactly circular. This is so because at first the ball got squished while we were cutting slices from it and second when we ran them over with the roller. While in traditional millefiori you would ideally want to avoid these effects, here they do not present a problem; distortions are even welcome as they produce a natural look, and that is our objective.

53. Fold together the inner end of the wings as shown. This way you make them three-dimensional and sturdier.

54. Make a small clamp from a piece of wire armature and stick the two inner edges of the wings together around it as shown. From the previous steps there should be enough clay where the wings are folded to accommodate the armature bit. Bake the wings in the oven. Baking time may be shorter than usual because the wings are quite thin. Wait for the wings to cool off and harden before you continue. It looks like a butterfly, does it not?

55. . . . so much so that we just could not resist!

56. Cut out two more slices of the remaining wing fruit. Put them on top of the dress as shown and wrap them around the shoulders of the fairy.

"Mirror, mirror on the wall, who's the fairiest of them all?"

57. Carefully insert the protruding wire bits into the back of the fairy to fasten the wings; you may want to exert counter-pressure by placing a finger on the belly. Use the clay shapers to smudge some clay around the wire bit and cover the joint between the back and the wing apparatus if necessary. Bake the fairy according to the clay manufacturer's instructions.

variations

Fairies feel at home everywhere; they are tiny enough to make a home out of most things, too.

Fairies look good around tiny things from nature such as pinecones, acorns, leaves, chestnuts, and berries.

This chubby troll barely managed to get his well-rounded moss-covered self into a pink fairy costume for the forest carnival.

chapter 5

MERMAIDS

Jambalini, the Mermaid

Every place on Earth is populated with magical creatures and mythical beasts. Just like the mountain forests and woods are teeming with all sorts of hopping, crawling, flying, impish water-fearing critters, the seas and the oceans are full of mer-folk—half-people, half-marine creatures, who swim like fish and rarely come ashore. A countless number of stories tell us of sailors who set sail toward distant shores, and on their voyage encountered and fell in love with the fairies of the sea-mermaids, beautiful sea-girls with the tail of a fish.

In this project we will practice sculpting the female human face and upper part of the body. Last but not least, we learn how to make the scaly tail of a fish. And you will finally find out what you can do with your seashell collection.

MATERIALS
- polymer clay in the following colors: dark blue, light blue, flesh, dark red, purple

TOOLS
- cutter
- taper-point clay shaper
- cup-round clay shaper

TIME FRAME
- 60 to 90 minutes (excluding baking time)

***Jambalini is** a beauty,*
Jambalini is a cutie.
She knows the secrets of the sea,
go with her and you will see
of the ancient ships the debris,
how clown fish roam free
and the sharks let them be.
She will show you how at the sea king's ball
you must dance with the water's flow.

Jambalini will tell you funny stories
of the quarrels of corals,
she will teach you how to surf the waves
and talk to the whales.
This lovely lady will stir your feelings,
give you a new emotion
of admiration and devotion to the ocean.
Then you will know that water is the magic potion
that keeps life in motion.

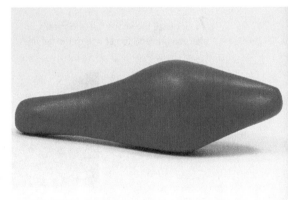

1. Fish, in case you didn't know, hatch from eggs just like chickens. So, roll out a fairly large (by fish standards) egg like the one shown.

2. Roll between the palms of your hands to get a short, thick snake without pointy ends. This is going to be the "mer" part of the mermaid, so pick your color wisely. Navy blue and silver (or even mixed together) are a good choice.

3. Roll on both ends to get a shape like the one shown—the bulky part in the middle will be the mermaid's hips and bottom, the elongated left side will be her tail, and the shorter tapering right side will be the mermaid's lower back.

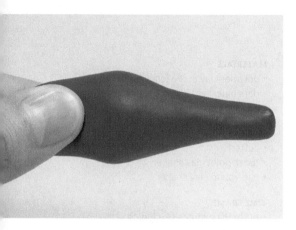

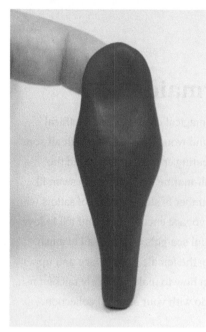

5. Here is the bulk of the mermaid's lower body. And now . . . to the fish tail.

6. Hold a ball of clay between your index finger and thumb, slightly askew, and roll until it becomes pointy. Do the same to the other side. You should end up with a shape similar to the one in the picture.

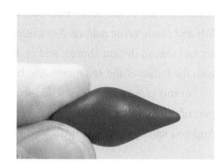

4. Squeeze on the area that will be the lower back to make a dent where the torso of the critter will soon sit.

8. Stick the first half of the fin to where the mermaid's feet look like where they would be. Repeat the last couple of steps to make the other half of the tail fin. Whatever side of the body you choose to stick them to—that will be the lower back side. If you think of the tail fins as feet, that would be the equivalent of the heel. We chose for this mermaid to be in a sitting position, because isn't this what mermaid's do all day long—be it on the beach or on a rocky shore? We never once knew a mermaid that did a day's work in her life. . . .

7. Squeeze the shape flat and gently sharpen one end to get half of the tail fin.

9. Put some roughly parallel lines on the tail fin as shown, using the first tool that looks as if it might do the trick: a needle, credit card, cutter, and box knife are a few choices.

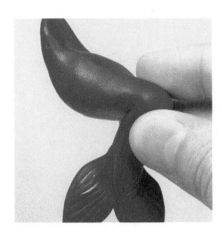

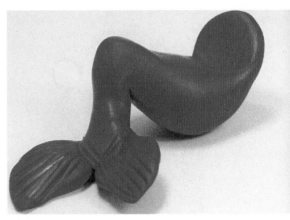

10. Bend the "legs" of the mermaid as shown to make the knees. While you bend the knees, these will widen, so squeeze as shown to correct for this.

11. The clay that gets displaced when you fold a piece of clay has to go somewhere; if you fold vertically it goes to the sides, if you fold horizontally it goes up and down. Gently squeeze the clay in—thus compacting in and getting rid of the unwanted spillover.

12. Here is the fish, but where is the girl? Think of the fish part as a dress that will be worn by the girl, except instead of high heels she is wearing flippers.

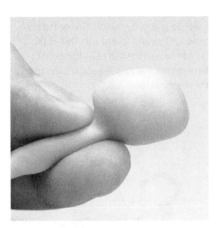

13. To make the face, we go through most of the same steps used in the fairy project. Put some clay on a basic armature bit, with an oval shape on the spoon end as shown.

14. Use a taper-point clay shaper to make eye sockets and extract a tiny, barely protruding nose from the face.

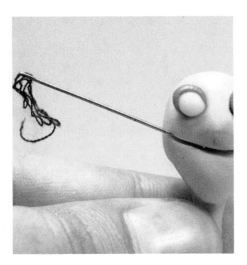

15. Here's the good old glow-in-the-dark ball (eyeball) wrapped in a squished snake (eyelid).

Pick a nonflesh color for the eyelid to make it look like the mermaid is wearing makeup. You can also use one of the glitter-effect clays.

16. Stick the eyes into their sockets and experiment by drawing a wide smile on the mermaid's face. Although a step later we correct this experiment, it is useful in that it gives us some idea of what the face would look like with a wide mouth. By drawing on the surface of the clay with a needle, you can sometimes get a preview of what would happen if you did this as opposed to that.

The crumpled-up thread hanging from the needle's ear is there not because it is pretty but because it helps you not to lose it. A work surface covered with multicolored pieces of clay and tools can sometimes be as dangerous as a haystack, when it comes to needles.

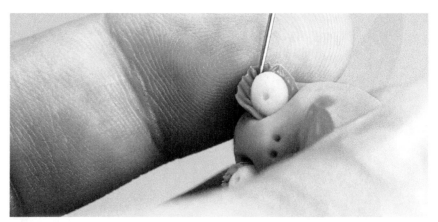

17. Close the mouth you opened in the last step and squeeze the cheeks so that the cheekbones stand out.

18. It is time for some needlework! Put two holes for the nostrils, two for the eyes, and make eyelashes by gently holding the back of the eyelids, as shown, and drawing with the pin.

Roll a tiny snake with two pointy ends out of lipstick-colored clay. Stick it under the nose, making sure to leave enough room for a delicate upper lip. Make the lower lip gradually thicker. Giving the mermaid full lips and a wide mouth ties the human face to the fish tail—fish tend to have similar mouths. A good reason to give the mermaid fuller lips.

19. Use the taper-point clay shaper to put a tiny dent at the corners of the mouth and on the upper lip.

20. Hold the mermaid by the neck and roll between your index finger and thumb until you get rid of any excessive chin that remains.

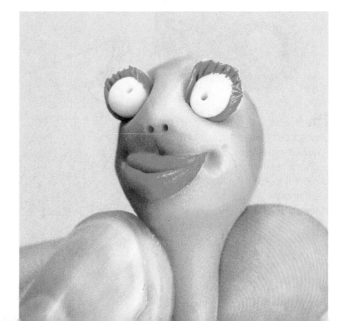

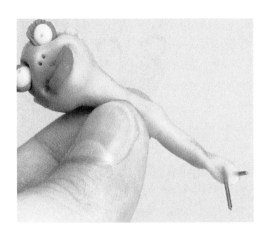

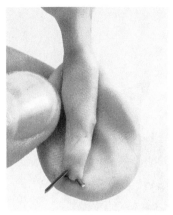

21. We now switch from the head to the torso. Put some more flesh on the bones of the mermaid as shown. Use the tips of your fingers and a clay shaper to smudge the seams that form when you put new clay on top of the old one.

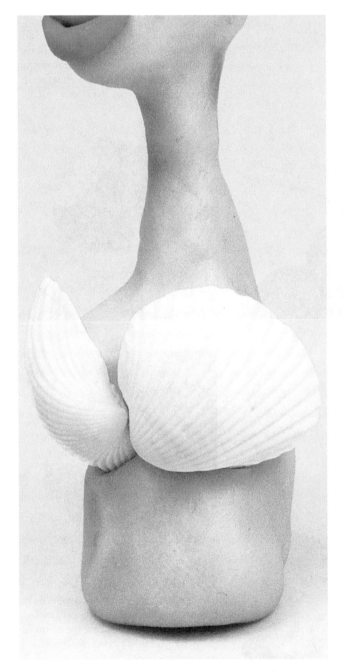

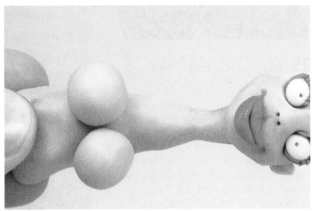

22. To make the bosom of the mermaid, stick two balls of clay to the body. Press on the upper part of each breast to smudge it into the torso.

23. Find two seashells of roughly identical size and use them, as shown, to make a bra for the mermaid. The "classic" white seashell works best. If, by chance, you have run out of seashells, two disks of clay will do the trick as well. If you have only one seashell—make an imprint on a lump of clay, bake the clay, and then use it as a mould to make the second one.

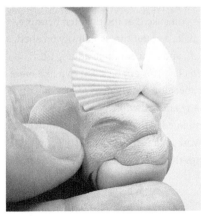

24. Cover the torso with a thin layer of light blue (pearl effect) clay.

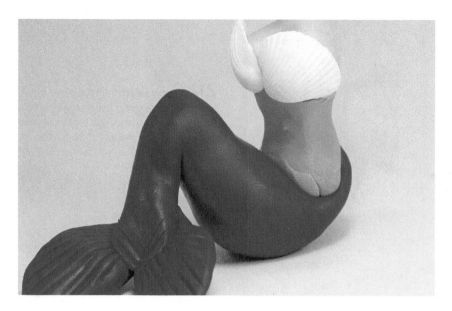

25. Stick the upper body to the lower body.

26. So far, so good. Note that we used the back of the clay shaper to make a dent between where the collarbones ought to be. That way, the mermaid looks thinner. The ear that materialized is made the same way as the ear of the fairy—a speck of clay with a small taper-point clay shaper hole in it.

27. Use a small tube to cover the tail of the mermaid with scales. Note that for this pattern you do not make full circles, so you need to push on the clay holding the tube slightly to one side. This particular tube is a broken off bit from an antenna. But do not go breaking your TV from the '80s just yet; first try using a pen's nozzle after you have removed the ink cartridge.

28. Here is how to hold the mermaid while you make the scales. There will be places you cannot reach—at the back and the bottom, where your fingers are.

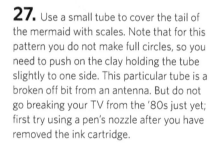

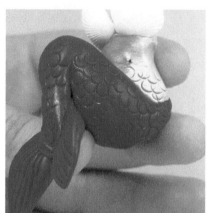

MULTIPLE BAKINGS

Polymer clay has the property to maintain its color and firmness as long as you bake it at the right temperature. You can therefore bake a critter that is halfway finished, wait for it to cool off, and then continue adding fresh clay over the baked clay. This enables you to make more complex creatures, because the chances of messing up parts that are already finished while you work on the other ones are eliminated; you can't squish an intricate tail fin while you work on a mermaid's hairstyle, and vice versa. Getting things right sometimes simply means not ruining them.

29. Place the mermaid on a work surface that can go into the oven—a ceramic tile in this instance. Put scales on the bald spots, where your fingers were. Bake the mermaid in the oven according to the clay manufacturer's instructions.

30. Make sure that the mermaid has enough forehead. In case she does not, put a lump of clay on top of the now-baked head and use a clay shaper to make it blend in.

31. Put two very thin arching snakes over the eyes for eyebrows.

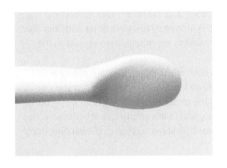

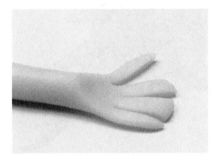

32. To make the mermaid's arm, follow the same procedure as the one we used for a fairy: Squeeze one end of a flesh-colored snake flat.

33. Using a cutter, separate the thumb first. The thumb is shorter and thicker, far-ther up on the hand, and at an angle to the fingers.

34. Cut out the individual fingers. This is called turning the mitten into a glove. The number of fingers is up to you; however, if you insist on playing by the book (certainly not this book), four fingers, instead of the recommended three, may require a wider palm and bigger hands, which sometimes makes a mermaid look like a mole. A sea mole, if you ever saw one, is a fascinating creature but not nearly as graceful as a mermaid.

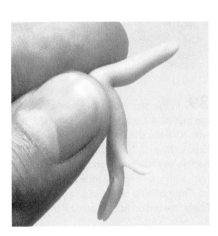

35. Spread out the fingers, and with the tips of your fingertips, slightly elongate them by gently pulling and squeezing at the same time. At this scale, every small pressure you apply matters. To round the fingers you only need to tap your index and thumb fingertips around them a few times.

36. Bend the arm at the elbow as shown. We will attach the upper arm to the torso as we did in the fairy project. For now, though, leave the arm at rest while we work on the mermaid's hair.

37. Hair is made up of pointy-ended snakes of different lengths and thicknesses. Think of each snake as a streak of hair that needs to be arranged in a hairdo. Because of the windy, open-air nature of the mermaid's dwelling, we opt for a disheveled hair, floating in the breeze.

Start by sticking the longest and thickest snakes to the skull first. Have most of them align in one general direction (that of the breeze), while leaving a few sticking out in different directions. These provide the backbone of the hair; we stick the shorter, thinner ones on top of them. Put the finer and tinier snakes around the forehead as shown. This reflects the true-to-life fact that at the beginning of one's hairline, the individual hairs are tinier and finer than the general hair; hence streaks of finer hair (small snakes) are thinner than streaks in the back of the hair (large snakes).

Make sure that all the streaks are pointy on both ends. When they are pointy at the lower end, it looks as if the mermaid got her hair all wet, not unreasonable given she swims in the sea to get around. When they are pointy on the upper end, you can seamlessly build them in between other streaks by putting the pointy end in the empty space between other streaks. That way the new streak of hair does not look plastered on top of the existing ones; it looks naturally lodged between them.

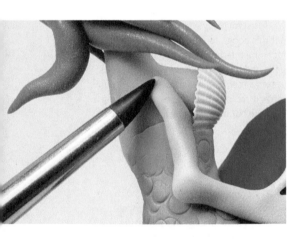  

38. Stick the arm to the torso and round the shoulder with a clay shaper.

39. In this step we curl up the hair of the mermaid, because eddies, circles, and whirlpool-like shapes add to the sea-life look. Hold your thumb under the streak of hair slightly touching it and push the tip back with your fingers a little until it curls up. The motion is one of sliding your index finger forward on top of your still thumb.

40. Build in purple streaks to match the mermaid's eyebrows. Notice how the purple streaks fits in because of their pointy ends.

41. Use the tip of a needle to draw a few individual hairs on the most prominent streaks in the front.

42. Here is your mermaid. Bake the finished character according to the clay manufacturer's instructions.

variations

Using the instructions on how to make a male upper body in the Centaur project in this book you can make a merman to keep the mermaid company. You can make mer any-old-thing, for that matter.

Another variation of the mermaid, with slightly different hairstyle.

This mermaid loves to tango with the sea horses. The concept that the fish tail is a dress was taken literally here.

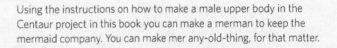

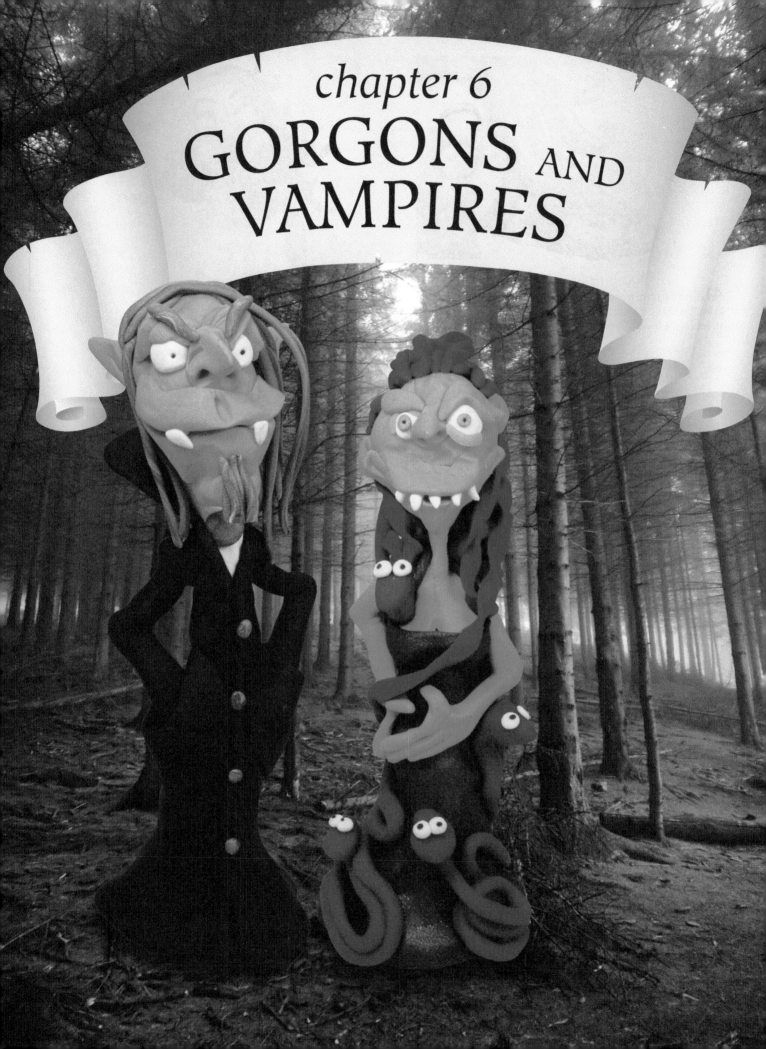

chapter 6
GORGONS AND
VAMPIRES

Medusa, the Gorgon and Branduff, the Vampire

This chapter deals with two creatures simultaneously, to demonstrate how with very little variation, a considerable difference of character can be achieved.

Gorgon Medusa was a sea nymph famous for her beauty. Poseidon, the sea god, courted her in a temple of Athena and Medusa kissed the ruler of the sea in the temple. Furious with such misbehavior, Athena punished Medusa by turning her into one of the ugliest creatures known to the world. It is said that she was so ugly that even a glimpse of her face turned men to stone.

What about Branduff the vampire? It is quite safe to say that nowadays he is the never-changing embodiment of evil and all kinds of life-sucking forces. A pure stereotype.

MATERIALS
- polymer clay in the following colors: green, black, white, orange, gold effect, silver effect, purple, blue
- baking foil

TOOLS
- linemen's pliers
- needle-nose pliers
- ceramic tile for work surface
- needle
- taper-point clay shaper
- cup-round clay shaper

TIME FRAME
- 2 hours (excluding baking time)

This is Medusa the Gorgon.
She is ugly as a creature from hell,
so ugly that there are no words to tell.
Her looks turn her visitors into stone
and she is always alone.
She has a secret wish—
to have other friends besides strange fish.
All this turned out to be a situation really bad
and the gorgon was really, really sad.

Little did she know
that in a far away mountain covered with snow,
someone to a vampire her portrait had shown.
The picture he saw, in his eyes was a glow.
He felt a feeling he'd forgotten long ago.
And so his love on Medusa he bestowed.
One day to her island he came . . .
"I am Branduff. Hello."

1. Make a pole of wire with a circular base. This is the armature for the gorgon. Make the same piece of armature for the vampire.

2. Cover the armature with baking foil. Press the foil stuffing at the appropriate places to make the curves of a woman's body.

3. Wrap baking foil around the vampire's armature. Make just a cone of foil. Compare the two wrapped armatures. You should be able to differentiate which one will be the gorgon and which one will be the vampire. Despite the difference in the slightly wider waist of the gorgon, the next two steps are the same for both characters.

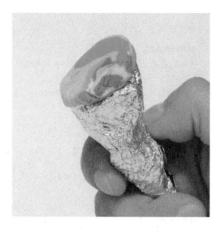

4. Place a disk of scrap clay under the body and put the creature's body on your work surface.

5. Roll a ball of foil. This is the scull of the gorgon. Make a heartlike shape for the skull of the vampire.

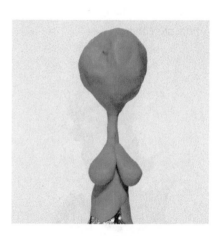

6. Cover the gorgon's head and neck with green clay. Don't smooth the clay coat. The uneven facial skin contributes greatly to the ugliness of the creature. Attach ears to the head. If you don't remember how the ears are made, return to chapter 1 and review the gnome's ears.

7. Add two droplets of green about 1" (2.5 cm) under Medusa's neck to make her breasts.

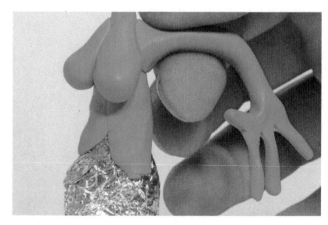

8. Cover the vampire's head with green clay and add pointy ears to his head. If more reference on pointy ears is needed, return again to chapter 1 and Rollieball. After the ears are in place, leave the vampire alone and devote your entire attention to the gorgon.

9. Make a thin hand and attach it to the body of the gorgon.

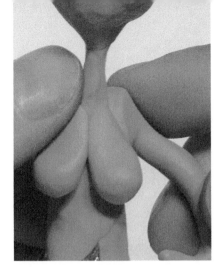

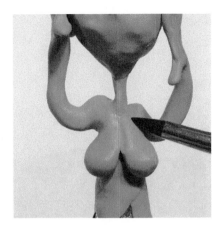

10. Support the side of the body with one hand and press with the index finger of the other hand as shown to form the shoulder.

11. Curve the hands up and attach them very lightly to the head. Repeat the previous three steps for the other hand. Use the taper-point shaper to smooth the places where the breasts and the hands are attached to the torso.

12. Roll two long black shoulder straps and put them in place.

13. Cover the gorgon's body with a black dress as shown. There might be arguments as to what is the most appropriate color for her dress, but black is always fashionable—even in the mythical dress code. Once the gorgon is dressed, lower the hands and place them in whatever gesture you choose.

14. Add two different-sized white eyeballs and place a green droplet between the eyes to make the nose.

15. Use the taper-point clay shaper to scratch the inside of the gorgon's nostril.

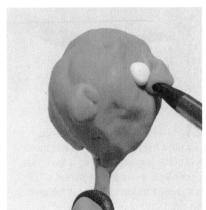

16. Add a randomly curved strip of green to form the lower lip.

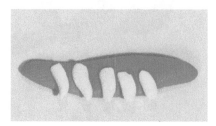

17. Make a green strip of clay for the upper lip and attach sharp jagged teeth to it.

18. Place the upper lip where it belongs, right under the nose and over the lower lip.

19. Add mouth corners to unite the upper and lower lips into a frightening grin. Make two orange eyelids. Put one as an upper eyelid for the left eye and the other as a lower eyelid for the right eye.

20. Make a second set of green upper eyelids and install them.

21. Make long flat strips of blue clay and twist them into spirals. This is the hair of the gorgon. Well, not actually hair; since Medusa has snakes instead of hair, this is dead snakeskin that still hangs from her head.

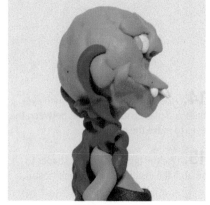

22. Start attaching blue strips to the lower back part of the gorgon's head.

23. Start adding the real snakes. The snakes are basically really long ropes of clay, each with a pointy end on one side and a fat snake head on the other side. Make sure that you attach the pointy end to the head and that the snakes curl nicely around the gorgon's body. Besides their classic function of scaring people, snakes function as a dress decoration here, too.

24. Make eyes for all the snakes.

25. Once all snakes are in place, add to the head another layer of blue spiraling strips to the top of the gorgon's head. Put an iris in each of the eyes. For a pupil, just poke a hole into each eye with a needle.

26. While the lady is baking, return to the vampire gentleman and add to his head a set of big eyelids.

27. Make a second pair of eyelids, only thinner this time.

28. Make and attach the eyeballs.

29. Cover the eyeballs with a third set of eyelids. Making three sets of eyelids creates the impression of wrinkled skin, something typical for the mature vampire.

30. Place a big green droplet between the eyes, the same as for Medusa's nose, only bigger.

31. Squeeze the nose to make it sharp.

32. Use a taper-point clay shaper to make the nostrils and attach the nose to the upper lip.

33. With a cup-round clay shaper, sculpt the outside of the nostrils.

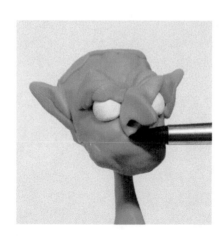

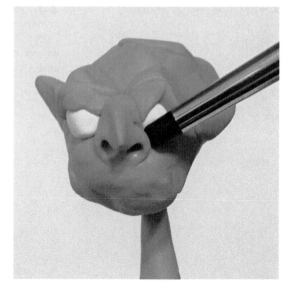

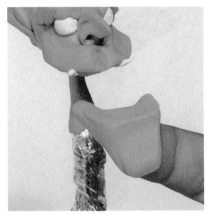

34. Make a fat upper lip. Sculpt it as shown with a taper-point clay shaper.

35. Attach the vampire's fangs to the upper lip.

36. Add the lower jaw.

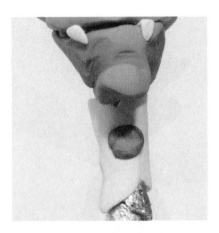

37. Curve the fangs down and the chin up.

38. Make a white strip as wide as your index finger and wrap it around the vampire's neck. This is the collar of his shirt.

39. Make a big gold clay button to hold the vampire's shirt collar.

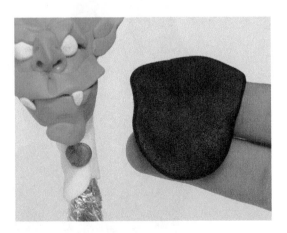

40. Sculpt a flat roughly rectangular piece of black clay to create the collar of his coat. Coats with high collars may be a little outdated, but vampires really like them.

41. Finish the entire coat. Be careful not to miss a single spot and cover the entire body of the vampire.

42. Make two long cylinders for the hands and attach them to the body. Make a long strip of black extending from the collar to the bottom of the coat and attach to it the silver clay buttons of the vampire. The silver buttons are actually really small balls of clay.

43. Form the shoulders, just like Medusa's shoulders. Black clay is often softer than the other colors of clay, so the shoulders can be formed simultaneously by pressing with both index fingers.

Fold the hands in the middle to form the elbows and attach the hands to the body.

44. Make two big flat crescents of black clay for the coat pockets. Cover the hands with the black crescents. This way it looks like the vampire has put his hands in his pockets.

ANCIENT TRICK

Making a humanoid creature that has put his hands in his pockets is one of the oldest known tricks in the book. It saves time and avoids having to sculpt the hands, which is sometimes a tedious task.

45. Add tiny black balls in the middle of the vampire's eyes for the pupils. Roll long, thin, gray snakes to create the vampire's hairstyle. Here goes Branduff the Vampire, hands in his pockets, looking handsome and feeling good. Bake the finished character according to the clay manufacturer's instructions.

variations

Gorgons and vampires make good couples. Here are two more lovebirds, who could not be happier than in each other's company.

Single gorgons are particularly vain. This one has her hair done at the snake charmer's practically every other day.

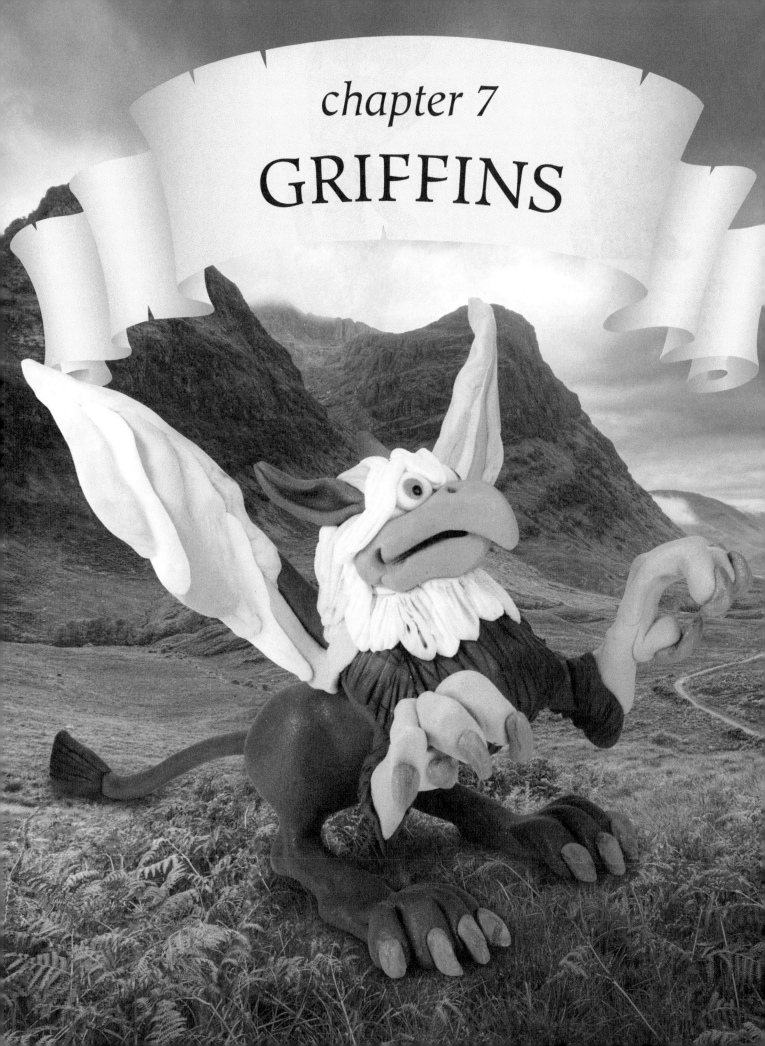

chapter 7
GRIFFINS

Orelav, the Griffin

The griffin is a majestic creature with the head, beak, and wings of an eagle, and the body of a lion. Griffins are also sometimes portrayed with a scorpion's or serpent's tail. They come from the ancient myths of the Middle East. Babylonians, Assyrians, Romans, Persians, and Greeks all featured griffins in their paintings, sculptures, and decorations. In Christian countries the Griffin motif also appears, most frequently as decoration of cathedrals and other buildings. If you look closely you will notice that a lot of gargoyles are in fact griffins. Heraldry is another favorite griffin's dwelling; coats of arms frequently feature some combination of griffins, swords, and shields.

In this project you will learn how to make armature for a winged four-legged beast, which is about as complicated as mythical beasts come—if you skip the snake for a tail, that is. You will get to practice most of the techniques you learned so far in this book, while getting acquainted with some aspects of the anatomy of lions and eagles.

MATERIALS
- polymer clay in the following colors: two browns, lemon yellow, dark yellow, white, green, two grays, silver, gold effect
- baking foil
- wire

TOOLS
- cutter
- taper-point clay shaper
- cup-round clay shaper
- pliers
- wire cutters
- ceramic tile
- needle
- pointy-ended instrument

TIME FRAME
- 60 to 120 minutes (excluding baking time)

Orelav the Griffin,
guardian of the divine,
is a creature noble and fine.
He is the keeper of treasures unseen,
protector of virtues and enemy of all sin.
This beast has a most wonderful nest
and appears on every important family crest.
Instead of eggs it lays sapphires

and according to learned friars
he has medicinal powers.
His nails scare the common cold
and one of his feathers mixed with gold
will even cure the bald.
Orelav is powerful and wise,
but to everyone's surprise
he is also very, very nice.

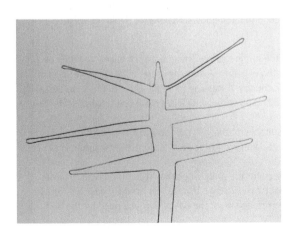

1. Fold a 39½" (100.3 cm) piece of wire in two. Proceed to fold as shown. The bit in the middle will support the griffin's neck; the first folds are his front legs, the second are his wings, and the third are his legs. The vertical lines in the center and the two loose ends in the lower part of the picture will be the tail. The exact measurements for the project shown here follow; however, keep in mind that they are arbitrary and you can change them if you please. Just remember that the griffin must have a neck, two front legs, two wings, two hind legs, and a tail. It is up to you how long these limbs will be. In our featured project, the first fold is at ¾" (1.9 cm) from the top. The second fold is 3" (7.6 cm) long. The space between the front legs and wings is ⅝" (1.6 cm). The wings are 4¼" (10.8 cm) long. The space between the wings and the hind legs is ¾" (1.9 cm). The legs are 3" (7.6 cm) long. The tail is 3½" (8.9 cm) long.

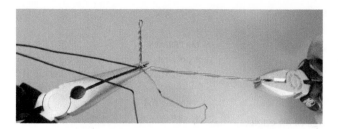

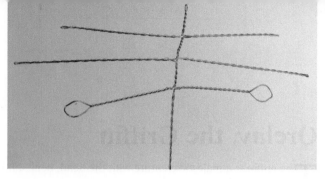

2. Hold the wire with the needle-nose pliers at the neck. With of the flat-nose pliers twist the two parallel wires around each other; proceed to do this with each two opposite pieces of wire. Twisting the wire gives your griffin's skeleton more strength and a little less flexibility, just enough to support all the muscle you are about to build.

3. When twisting the wire for the hind legs, leave a small loop at the end. When this circle is covered with clay it will become a foot and will help the mythical creature stand firmly on the ground.

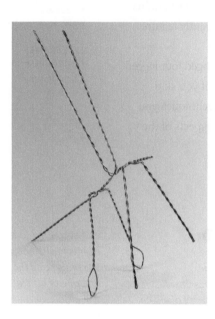

4. Fold the wings up. Fold the front and hind legs down from the spine and tail. Now you have a clearly visible bone structure for the critter. Straighten the back of the griffin as shown. The legs have to be bent in the middle to form knees.

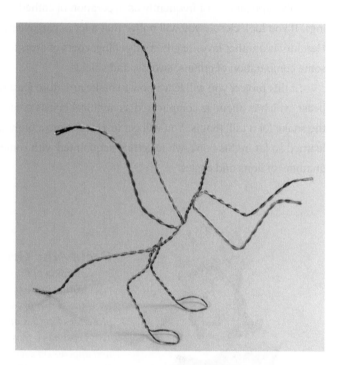

5. Note that these, unlike human legs, bend forward. Then fold the feet in a way to ensure that the griffin has both feet on the ground.

Fold the wings in a direction opposite to the front legs. Generally the wings have an S shape.

Proceed to bend the wire of the front legs. Be sure that the griffin has shoulders. They are created by making the wire swerve a little and not come straight out of the "backbone." This is the first fold. Make a second fold for elbows. Make a third fold for wrists.

6. Wrap baking foil around the griffin's spine. The quantity of baking foil defines what physique and posture your griffin will have. Amassing more foil at the lower part of the body will make the griffin look chubby. Amassing more foil close to the shoulders will make the griffin look muscular and powerful, which is what these creatures are more famous for.

Mix a color that you find suitable for the griffin's body. In most cases this is some shade of brown. Brown looks good on griffins because essentially the griffin is a creature with a lion's body.

The quantity of clay you need for the body when making a griffin with the exact measurements we offer is about 7 oz (200 g). In case you want to make a different size of griffin, here is the approximate size of the ball of clay you need for the body in relation to the skeleton.

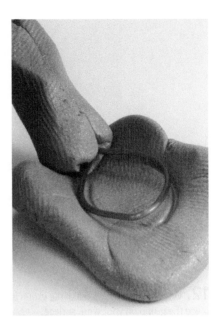

7. Start covering the griffin's body with clay as shown.

8. Be sure to cover the following parts: torso, tail, front legs up to the elbows, hind legs, and the section of the wings, which is closest to the body.

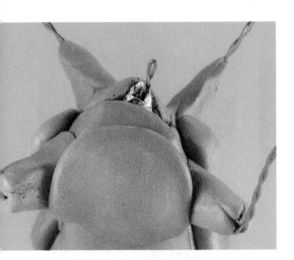

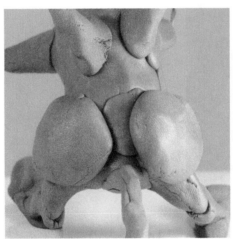

9. After the entire body is covered with a first rough coat of clay, add two squished balls of clay to the hips, two to the shoulders and one to the chest. This is how we build volume.

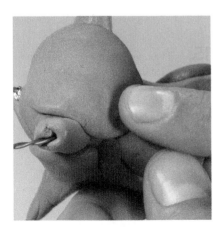

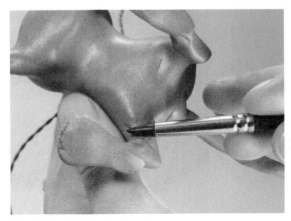

10. Blend the pieces of clay that cover the body. Start to do that with your fingers and use a clay shaper for the hard-to-reach places, as well as for finer work.

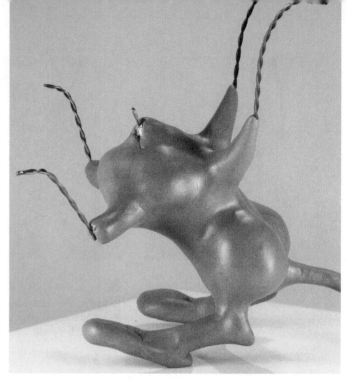

11. To shape the heel bone, squeeze between your index finger and thumb as shown.

12. When the body and tail of the griffin are smooth enough, place the griffin on your work surface.

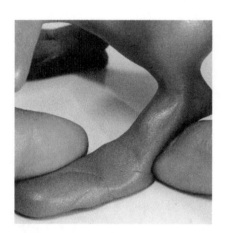

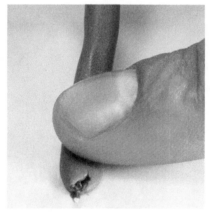

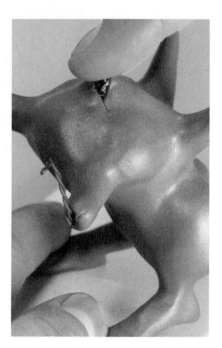

13. Press gently on the feet and tail to attach the griffin to the work surface. This makes turning the griffin and working on all sides much easier.

14. Pull back on the body while holding the feet of the griffin firmly to the ground to straighten his posture. While we did give the creature a skeleton the whole structure is still wobbly and flexible, so you may need to straighten it from time to time.

15. Roll four droplets of clay for the hind leg's toes. Do the same for the other leg.

16. Attach the droplets/toes to the hind paw. Their round front end must touch the work surface. It does not matter how far the thin end reaches as long as it is does not touch the leg.

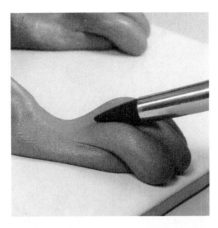

17. Gently press the pointy ends of the droplets to the paw. Smoothen this point with your finger first and then with the taper-point clay shaper.

18. Use a mixture of lemon yellow, dark yellow, glow-in-the-dark, and gray for the front legs. Start covering the front legs from the elbows to the end with that mixture.

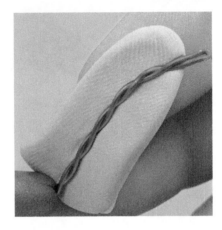

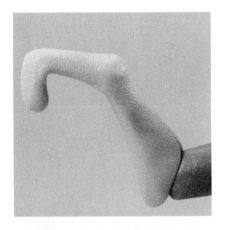

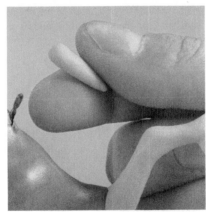

19. Cover the hand and the wrist and proceed to leave a piece of clay extending a bit farther; this piece will be one of the griffin's fingers. Bend that piece down at a 90-degree angle. Continue and make droplets as shown for the other fingers.

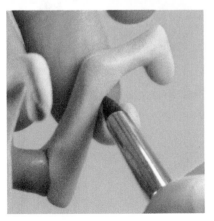

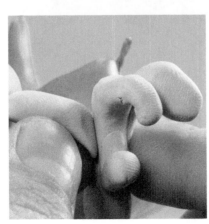

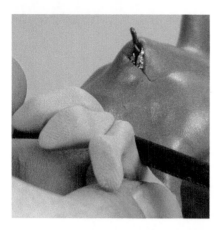

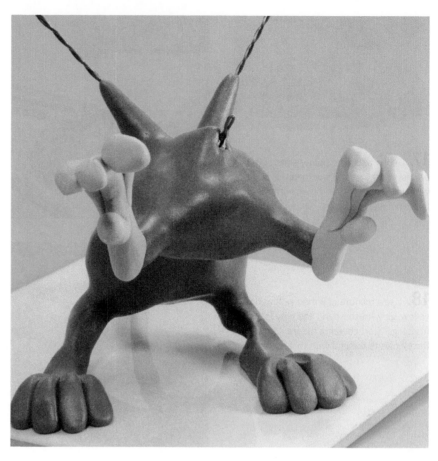

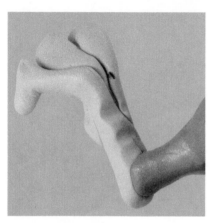

20. Make two dents with the back part of the taper-point clay shaper. Always remember that your tools have two ends, not just when your ears itch. Even though one of the ends is only intended as a hilt, there are still possibilities to use that end as a tool.

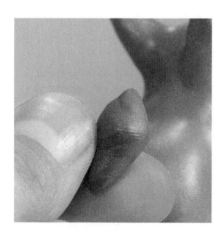

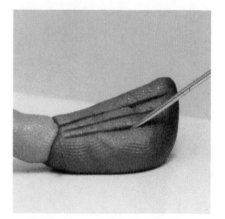

21. Prepare half a block of brown clay. Since it is for the mane, mix a brown color that is darker than the one you use for the griffin's body. Make a tassel for the end of the tail. What makes tassels particularly fun is that they are something that lions and donkeys have in common. Detach the tail very carefully from the work surface and add the tassel. Attach the tail to the work surface again. Scrape some individual hairs with a needle.

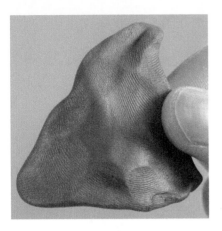

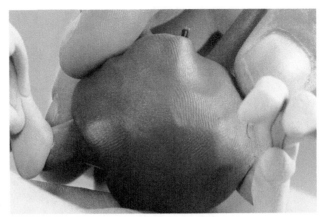

22. Make a triangular shape for the mane's front part. Wrap it around the upper part of the body.

23. Make a strip of that same brown clay and wrap it around the elbows. It covers the part where the green of the claws and the brown of the body are joined.

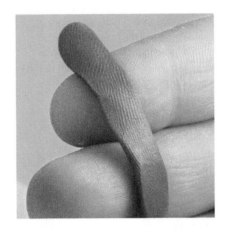

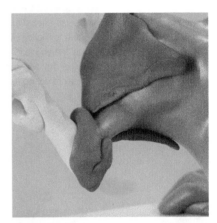

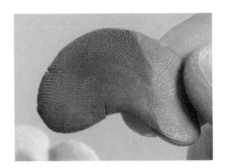

24. Make a shape like the one in the picture for the collar of the lion's mane.

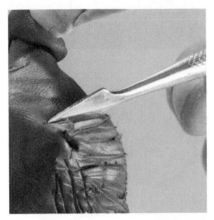

25. Gently detach the entire creature from the work surface. At this stage, you need to hold the creature in your hand to achieve the desired effect. Draw some individual hairs on the mane and at the elbows with a pointy-ended instrument of your choosing. Attach the entire creature to the ceramic tile again.

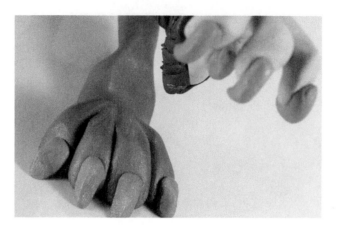

26. Make small gray droplets for the claws. Be sure to attach claws to all of the fingers. After the claws are attached and the critter is again on the tile, it is time to bake the creature. Since this is a rather complex figure, with a lot of limbs, it is getting increasingly difficult to make new bits without ruining the ones you already made. When we bake there will be no more accidental "dislocations" or broken nails on the critter. After baking, make sure to allow the clay to cool off and harden before you continue.

27. Cover half of the wings with white clay. Avoid using pure white. Any combination of light gray, white, white mixed with gold, or white mixed with beige will work well. If you observe a bird with white feathers, such as an eagle, you will notice that not all the feathers look white. Imitate nature.

28. Start adding feathers on top of the mane. After a collar of feathers is ready, add a piece of very light gray that will function as a skull.

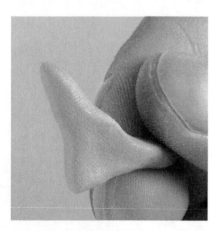

29. Make a small green triangle for the lower part of the beak as shown.

30. Turn the tip up.

31. Press from both left and right with your thumbs to make an edge in the middle.

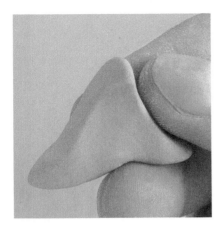

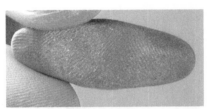

32. Make a larger triangle of the same color for the upper part of the beak. Press on it from both sides as shown to come up with the necessary shape.

33. Attach the upper beak jaw to the skull. Bend the tip down to obtain the characteristic eagle nose.

34. Cover the skull with some more feathers. After it is covered, add a feather in the middle that is considerably thicker than the others. For a middle reference point use the ridge in the middle of the beak. Add two glow-in-the-dark balls of clay on both sides of that feather for the eyes.

35. Make a flat, elongated, oval brown shape. Use clay in the same color as the one you used for the body. Gently squeeze both ends inward. Make the ends pointy. The end result should look like a canoe—this is the griffin's ear. Make a second ear.

36. Attach the ears right behind the eyes.

37. Add some more feathers. Stick some of the feathers close to the foundation of the ears to give the ears better support.

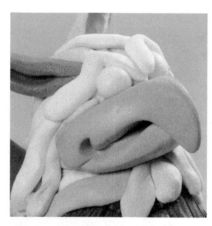

38. Add eyebrows on top of the eyeballs. Use the cup-round shaper to further shape the griffin's beak as shown.

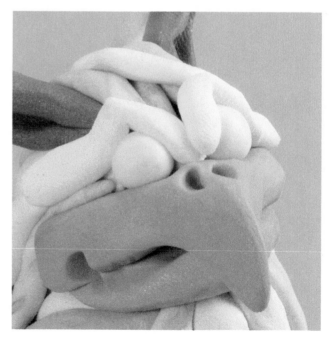

39. Make two holes for the nostrils, using the taper-point clay shaper. Flared nostrils, perked ears, and the fact that the griffin is standing on his hind legs are all elements that contribute to giving the creature his alert and energetic look, as befits a magnificent beast, guardian of treasures.

40. Return to the wings. Cover them with clay entirely. Make the end pointy.

41. Now is the penultimate stage of the project—the wings. There are several ways to make decent wings. You can make them feather by feather, which is the best way but takes forever and a day. The other ways are mostly creating the impression of wings. Here we will create that impression by using different alternating colors and S-like shapes.

Make a curved strip of light gray. Attach one end to the feathers of the head. Attach the other end to the wing. Press the middle of the strip to the wing.

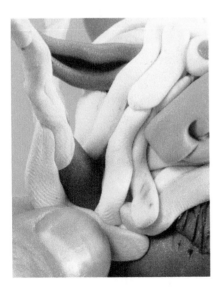
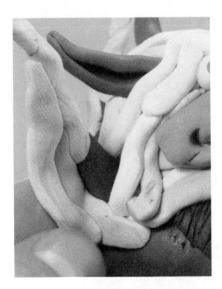
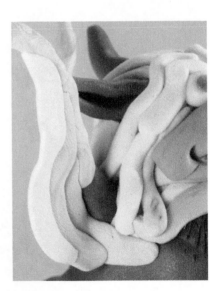

42. Make a slightly longer strip of white mixed with gold and attach it to the previous strip. The next strip you attach must be white. Follow that order of colors once more to finish the wing. Follow the same sequence of colors for the other wing.

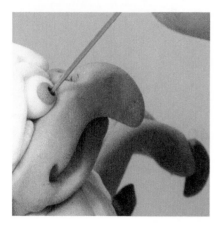

43. Make a small ball of silver clay, flatten it and place it in the middle of the eyeball. Make a smaller ball of black clay, flatten it and place in the middle of the silver eye. Take a needle and put a deep hole in the middle of the black part of the eye.

44. Take again your pointy-ended tool and give the feathers some texture.

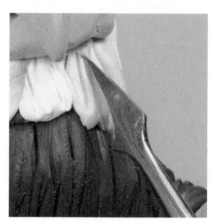

Voilà!

variations

A compact design—
the sitting griffin.

The Rare Snake-tailed Griffin
Note that the cobra snake design can also be used for the gorgon.

The Bald-Eagle Griffin

The phoenix, the fiery bird that bursts into flames and then rises to live again from the ashes. They are typically portrayed as chicken-like birds, but there is no reason not to go for the ducklike look.

A griffin who was turned into a gargoyle by the gorgon.

chapter 8

THE SPHINX

The Sphinx

The sphinx is an ancient being with the powerful body and bold heart of a lion and the handsome head and sharp wit of a man. He can sit for ages in a faraway land waiting for a random passerby to test with his riddles. The famous riddle of the sphinx goes like this:

What creature walks on all fours at dawn, on two legs at noon and at three at dusk? The answer is—the human being; babies craw on all fours before they learn to walk, grown-ups walk straight up on two legs, and old people sometimes use a cane.

Now you are prepared to meet the sphinx! The Egyptian look was chosen for this project, with the lying posture of the big-pawed lion with a pharaoh's head. The Great Sphinx of Giza near the pyramids is the inspiration.

MATERIALS
- polymer clay in the following colors: yellow, brown, silver, gold, dark green, flesh, black, glow-in-the-dark/white
- baking foil

TOOLS
- cutter
- taper-point clay shaper
- cup-round clay shaper
- sculpting tool

TIME FRAME
- 30 to 60 minutes (excluding baking time)

Hey diddle-diddle

here for you is a riddle:
What can reach Orion first?
A fantasy or an illusion?
What is your conclusion?
Yes, this is a riddle not a delusion.
This is the best one we have in our pockets.
This riddle we know from the Sphinx,
the one and only Sphinx who liked riddles
better than drinks.

The one that had, for a pet, a lynx.
The guy that never blinks—that is the Sphinx.
He is the one who wanted to know what everyone thinks,
who enjoyed writing letters with green ink and hated everything pink.
And since we have his permission and links we present you a portrait of the Sphinx.

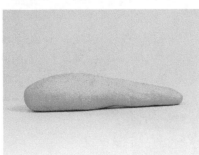

1. Crumple up some baking foil to form a shape like the one shown; flat underneath and oval on top. This will be the inside of the lion's body.

2. Cover the foil with yellow-brown clay (mixture of random parts of yellow and brown clay).

3. This is the torso of the lion; push down on it harder in the middle to make the back arch. Notice the small bump at the upper right corner—this is an air pocket. To deflate it, poke it with a needle and press with your fingers until the clay sticks to the foil.

4. To make the front legs of the lion's body, roll out a thick snake roughly shaped like a club or baseball bat.

89

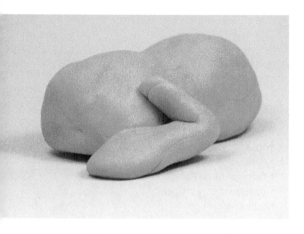

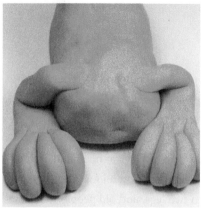

5. Bend the leg in and stick it to the front of the creature. Both upper and lower parts should stick to the torso, with the paw slightly protruding.

6. Make several raindrop-like shapes and stick them to the upper front part of the leg to form the paw. You already know how to do this from the griffin project. Use your fingers and a taper-point clay shaper to smudge the toes into the paw and the leg at the shoulder.

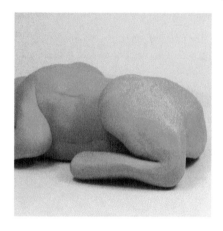

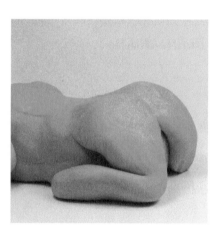

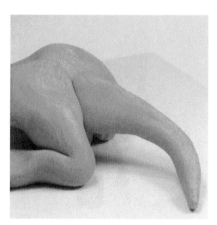

7. For the hind legs we follow essentially the same series of steps, only this time the leg is made out of a larger shape, the thick part of which has been squished a little flat. Bend that shape in the middle and stick it to the torso as shown.

8. Again, smudge with your fingers and a clay shaper.

9. To make a tail, roll out a thick snake, slightly tapering to one end, and stick it to the bottom of the sphinx as shown. Use a clay shaper to eliminate the seams.

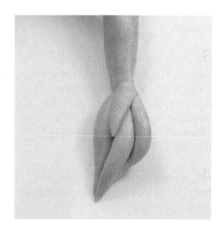

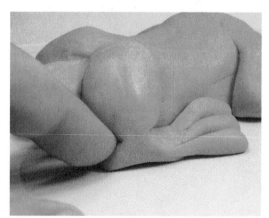

10. Put a tassel at the end by piling a few short snakes on top of one another. You can draw a few individual hairs with a needle on each snake.

11. Push with your finger and nail to give the lion a heel.

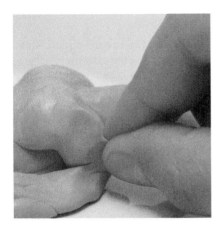

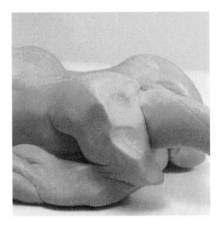

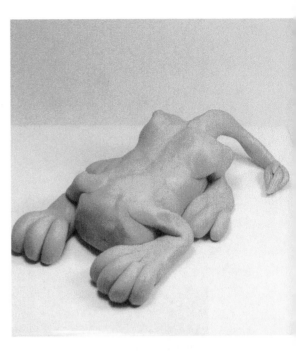

12. A lion is a furry beast, so do a couple of squeezes as shown to create the illusion of fur.

13. Here is the result of three such squeezes.

14. Here is what the sphinx's body looks like so far.

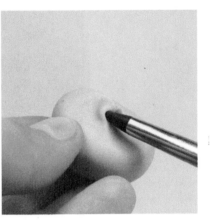

15. Next, we turn to the head. Roll out a ball of clay and push with your thumbs while holding with your index fingers until you get two dents with a ridge in the middle.

16. Push on the ridge to define where the nose ends.

17. Make two holes for the nostrils, using the taper-point clay shaper. Notice how the displaced clay forms the outside of the nostril. Use the cup-round clay shaper to define the nostrils.

18. This is an exploratory step, like the one in the mermaid project. Using the tip of the cup-round clay shaper and its handle, draw eyes, a mouth, and eyebrows to see what the face would potentially look like. A sphinx is a cunning creature, so a round, childish, naive-looking face does not fit in the picture. A skinnier face with finer features is the better choice.

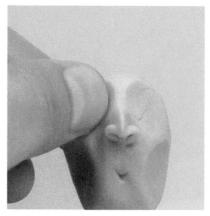

19. Perform two squeezes on the cheeks as shown to make them "hollow." Do the same for the eyes; in the process you will destroy the features drawn in the previous step, which was precisely the point. You can clearly see the marks left by the fingers on the right side of the face. The effects of the four dents we just put is that the space between them looks like protruding cheekbones. The cheeks will be hollow and the eyes will be sunken.

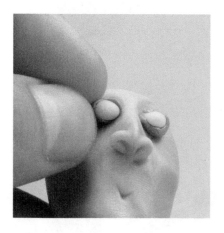

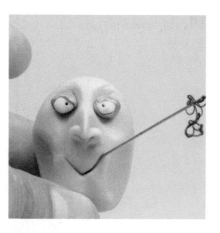

20. Make eyes by wrapping a silver snake squished flat around an egg-shaped glow-in-the dark piece of polymer clay. Stick the wrapped egg-shaped eyes to the face horizontally and lightly pinch the corner of the eye.

21. Draw a mouth again. Let us hope this time it will remain.

22. Make the corners of the mouth by pressing with the tip of the taper-point clay shaper.

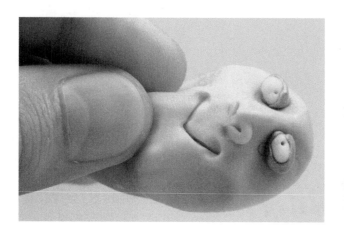

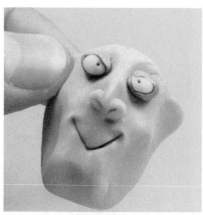

23. Pinch as shown to make a cleft chin.

24. Pull the ears out of the body as shown.

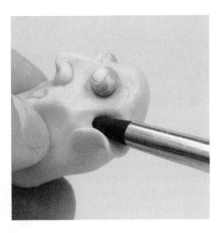
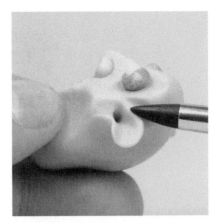

25. Fold the lower part of the ear up a little to form what resembles an earlobe. Put a hole in the ear with the taper-point clay shaper. Delimit the ear from the top. Make the ear pointy.

26. Attach two eyebrows made out of black clay snakes. Notice the two very tiny horizontal snakes in the corner of each eye; this is supposed to look like Egyptian makeup. To reinforce the makeup effect, draw two vertical lines with the needle under each eye. Put a black triangle for a goatee on the cleft chin. Roll out a flesh-colored snake and put it on the smile of the sphinx for a lower lip.

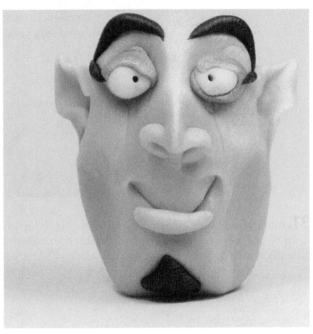

27. In this step, the dark shadows show where to place the two dents—one right under the nose of the sphinx and the other under the lower lip.

28. Roll out a ball of green clay, squish it flat, and thin it out while holding it between your thumb and middle and index fingers. Put this coat collar behind the sphinx's head as shown, right under the ears.

29. Wrap the green coat around the head as shown. Make a second, slightly larger coat of a clay mixture that has more brown in it, and wrap it around the green one. Stick the wrapped head on the body as shown.

30. Leave the lion's body and the human head to get used to each other for a while.

Roll out several alternating gold and silver snakes and stick them next to each other, as if you are building a raft. Using a roller or a tube, gently press on the raft to flatten it. Be careful not to make the raft too thin. It should be about as thick as the cover of a hardcover book. Cut off the ragged ends, but keep them.

31. Pull together the uneven ends of the waste that remain from the raft to form a fanlike structure, and pull on one of the gold bits to extract a tiny dangling in the center. We will place this atop the sphinx's head, like a nurse's cap, only a bit more royal.

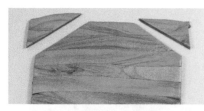

32. Cut off the two corners of the squished raft as shown.

33. Use a sculpting tool to round all the edges until you get a shape that is roughly semicircular.

34. Stick the two corners that you cut off two steps ago on both sides of the neck as shown.

35. Make a decorative shield by putting a wriggling yellow snake and two straight ones on top and to the sides of a squished raindrop-like shape.

36. Stick the cap on top of the sphinx's hat as shown. Notice that it is not completely flat but curved outward.

37. Turn the sphinx around and stick the squished raft to the back of the head as shown. The largest contact area should be on the sphinx's neck and it should be joined with the tip of the nurse's cap. Notice that the striped semicircle is not completely flat but curved with its lower right-angled corners pointing forward.

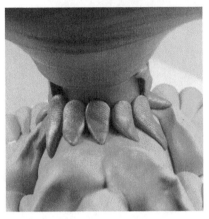

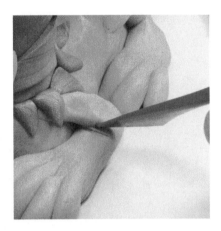

38. Roll out about a dozen droplike shapes and stick them around the neck of the sphinx to make a lion's mane. To make a pharaoh's goatee for the sphinx, stick a few balls of silver and black clay to each other and roll them between your fingers to pack them a little, then stick the ornament on the goatee we gave the creature before.

39. Use a sculpting tool to make two creases on the legs.

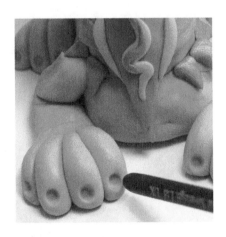

41. Behold the enigmatic sphinx! That is before he catches you unprepared, with one of his riddles. Note that the golden wriggling ornament on the breast of the sphinx has changed to silver over the last few steps. How this happened is a mystery even the great sphinx cannot unravel.

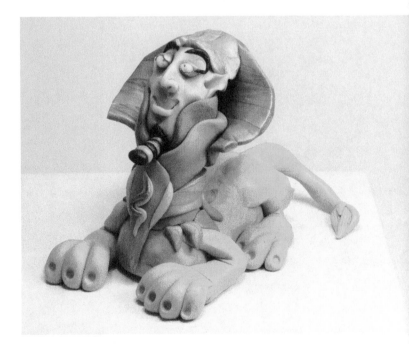

40. Using the handle tip of the clay shaper, put holes on each toe. You can also make claws, just like those of the griffin.

chapter 9
UNICORNS

Igrif Belcon, with the Unique Horn

The unicorn is one of the best-known mythical characters. His magical prowess aside, the unicorn's appearance is that of a horse with a single straight horn in the middle of the forehead.

MATERIALS
- polymer clay in the following colors: white, white glitter effect, flesh, gold
- baking foil
- wire

TOOLS
- cutter
- taper-point clay shaper
- cup-round clay shaper
- pliers
- wire cutters
- needle

TIME FRAME
- 60 to 120 minutes (excluding baking time)

Igrif Belcon is a unicorn.

His magical abilities are inborn.
No one can stop the unicorn, even a wall of stone.
This magic horse can take you to the moon,
he can read secret wizard scripts from morning to noon.
He can also talk, and if you take him for a walk
maybe he will find your long-lost gold treasure sock,
or show you how to domesticate a hawk.
And if your step is light in the night
when there is no light
and the unicorn is by your side
maybe you can catch a glimpse
of the outlandish dances of fairies and imps.

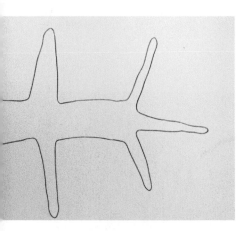

1. From a close distance you might be fooled into thinking that this is one of the giant land drawings in Nazca, Peru, that can only be seen from an airplane. Rub your eyes and take a second look—it is only the armature folding for the unicorn project. The rightmost end will be the head, the first set of perpendicular folds are for the front legs, the second set for the hind legs, and the loose ends (leftmost) are for the tail.

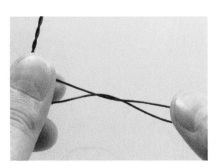

2. Hold the armature at the intersection with one of your hands while you twist with the other one.

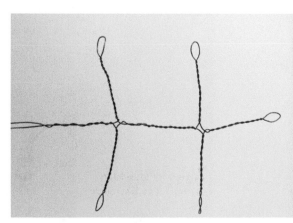

3. Here is the two-dimensional schematic; essentially it is the same one as the one for the griffin. The difference is in the way you fold it in the third dimension.

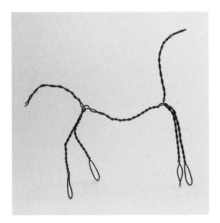 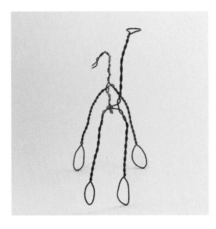 

4. Fold the armature as shown. The skeleton should be able to stand upright on its own. The skeleton does not need to be perfect—it will be all covered with clay, so you can correct for deviations from your mental image of the ideal horse by adjusting the quantity of clay that you put on the bones of the unicorn.

5. Wrap foil around the skeleton to create some volume. Apply foil for the neck and belly only.

6. Start covering the skeleton with a mixture of white, flesh-colored, and white glitter-effect clay. The flesh clay gets absorbed by the whites so you cannot really see it as such; its purpose is to offset the chalk-white color of the white and give it more translucency.

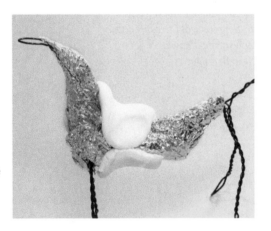 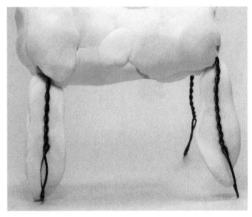

7. Here is the skeleton covered with a first rough coat of clay.

 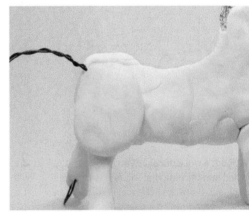

8. Horses, to which the unicorn is related, have a very powerful chest and hind legs. This is why we add more mass to these parts of the body. Place two squished disks of clay on each side of the unicorn's bottom as shown.

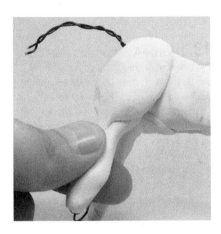

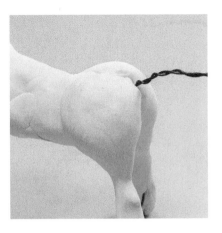

9. Smudge the clay disks as shown into the surrounding clay. Make sure to push on the outer edges without flattening the bulging muscles you made in the last step. You may already recognize this technique from the griffin project.

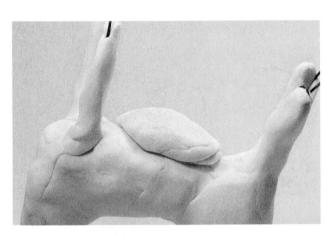

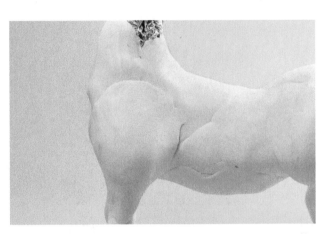

10. A horse's belly is particularly round—like a barrel. Make sure to use more clay as necessary to achieve that effect. Use a squished clay ball, like the ones for the hind legs. One could alternatively put a thicker tin foil core inside in the first place.

11. Use the same volume-adding technique to build stronger front legs and chest.

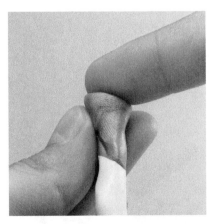

12. Wrap a piece of gold clay around the lower part of each leg to make the hooves. Push on the bottom of the hoof to flatten it, while at the same time holding it with your index finger and thumb. Give the hooves a roughly conic shape; imagine the tip of the cone is somewhere in the unicorn's leg.

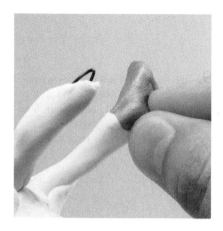

13. Pinch the hoof to make a "heel" for the unicorn. At this stage do not worry if the hoof has climbed up the leg too much; you will get a chance to correct this at a later stage, by wrapping a thin white sheet around the excess hoofage. Make an edge as the one shown on the hind legs of the unicorn—think of it as a sharp knee pointing backward.

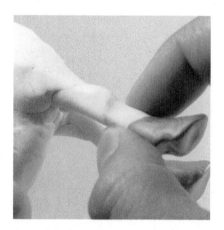

14. Gently squeeze under the knee and above the knee, to make it stand out.

15. Smooth all the seams, using your fingers and taper-point clay shaper, and put the unicorn in the oven for a first baking. If the armature does not reach all the way down to the bottom of the hoof, bake the unicorn lying down, so that it will not be crushed by its own weight while baking.

16. Take the unicorn out of the oven and let it cool off before you continue work.

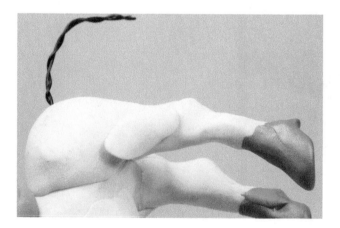

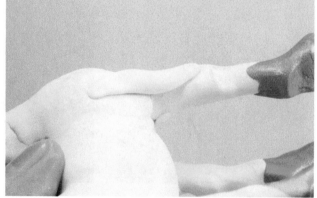

17. You held and rotated the unicorn a lot before baking, so it lost some of the volume it should have; inevitably the clay gets compressed. Now you can hold the unicorn any way you like, so it is a good time to make up for all the lost volume by adding squished sheets of clay here and there, as shown, and smudging them into the surrounding clay with fingers and a clay shaper.

18. Roll out a short, fat snake of the size shown.

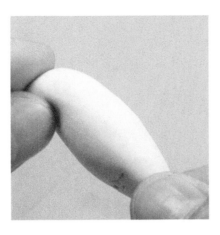

19. Bend the nozzle down as shown.

20. Stick a small ball of clay under the nozzle for a lower jaw.

21. Squeeze with your thumbs and index fingers as shown. In the picture, the finger hold is shown on the left side and the effect of the squeeze is visible on the right.

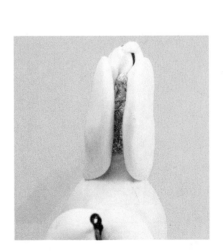

22. Put two disks of clay on each side of the head for cheeks. Connect the lower jaw to the head as shown. Do the same with the cheeks. The head is now ready to be attached to the neck, which we will now make.

23. To cover the neck, roll out a snake, squish it flat, and stick it frontally to the backbone as shown.

24. Make two egglike shapes and squish them flat. Put them on both sides of the neck, narrower end down as shown. Stick them to each other at the back and go over the seams with your fingers and clay shaper.

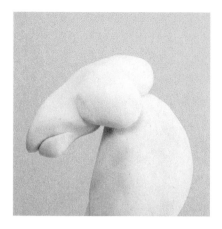

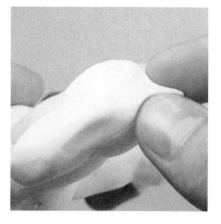

25. Attach the head to the neck as shown by gently spreading the cheeks and then pushing them back in.

26. Extract an ear out of the head as shown. You have to squeeze in a perpendicular plane to make the ear narrow.

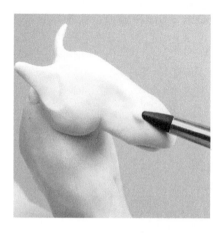

27. Use the clay shaper to give the unicorn flaring nostrils, and while you are at it, poke two holes in the ears.

28. Using the clay shaper, press on top of the ear as shown. Pinch the tip of the ears to give the unicorn an alert look.

29. Make an eye socket with a rotating motion of the taper-point clay shaper. Wrap a flattened snake around an eyeball and put it inside the socket. Note that the eyelid has to be thicker and wider this time, so as to cover all of the eyeball but the front. Draw an eyebrow and poke a hole in the eye with a needle. Repeat these steps for the other eye or make an eye patch for the first pirate unicorn in mythical world's history.

30. Wrap a piece of gold clay around the tail armature to cover it. Using the hair-streak technique that you are familiar with from previous projects, give the tail some volume.

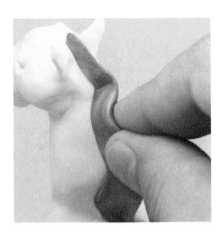

31. For the mane put a squished snake along the back of the unicorn's neck and squeeze to make it wavy (similarly to what we did for the hind leg of the sphinx). Use the tip of the needle to draw some individual hairs on the mane.

32. It is time to look at the big picture again, as the unicorn will be finished very soon. Look at the unicorn and try to think about what else needs to be done, or can be improved, before we attach the horn. Often when you focus on the particular detail of a critter (or just about anything else) the big picture gets blurred, so it helps to just take a step back, leave it to sit for a little bit and then return to work with a fresher mind and a keener eye.

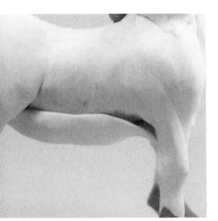 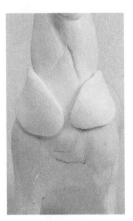 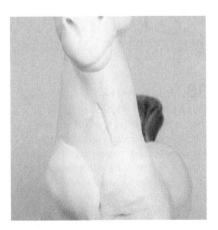 

33. The second look showed that the creature needs even some more muscle on its chest and belly.

34. As these are the finishing stages of the project, you will not be touching the surface of the unicorn for much longer (thus inadvertently but inevitably ruining any finer surface detail), so now is the time to be superficial and add spots and eliminate unwanted seams between the different lumps of clay.

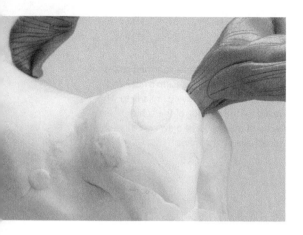

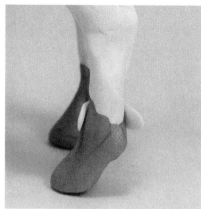

35. We made the spots by mixing in minuscule quantities of blue and gray clay with the white-glitter-flesh mixture we used for the body.

36. Put a white ankle bracelet around the hooves that sprawl too far up. Use fingers and a clay shaper to blend its upper side into the leg.

37. Add a mouth corner to join the upper and lower jaw. Put a tiny goatee underneath the lower jaw and draw some hairs on it.

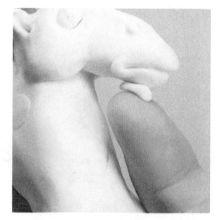

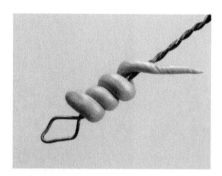

38. We saved the best for last! To make the unique horn, wrap a snake around a basic armature bit as shown, then gently roll between your index finger and thumb to tighten up and sharpen the horn. The armature bit has to be without a fork (cut off any loose ends). Make sure to cover the whole armature bit with clay and leave some in excess so that you can make the horn sharp. Bake the horn; after it cools off, stick the spoon end to the forehead of the unicorn. Bake the whole critter according to the clay manufacturer's instructions.

variations

Now that you have mastered how to make a humanlike and a horselike figure, you can combine your powers into one and make rider characters.

The unicorn is not really a beast of burden. This is why he is a little irritable when a damsel in distress asks him to carry her over a large puddle of water.

Pegasus, the winged flying horse, is a good buddy of the unicorn. To make Pegasus, you need an armature that has one extra set of limbs; the twisted wire in step 3 consists of one long horizontal line, again, and three (instead of two) vertical ones.

To make the wings, bend the middle limbs up, and cover with flat sheets of clay (shown in blue here). Then do a first baking at the same stage that we baked the unicorn. After you have baked once, start covering with white snakes squished flat as shown on the back and front of the wings.

chapter 10
CENTAURS

Abraxas, the Centaur

To make a centaur you need to know two things—how to make a horse's body and how to make a male human torso. You are practically halfway there because making a horse's body was covered in the unicorn project. The only minor difference is in the armature. The armature for the centaur should take into account the fact that he has got a longer body and an extra pair of limbs—the human hands.

MATERIALS
- polymer clay in the following colors: dark brown, reddish brown, flesh, gold, light green, silver
- baking foil
- wire

TOOLS
- cutter
- taper-point clay shaper
- cup-round clay shaper
- cutter
- pliers
- wire cutters
- needle

TIME FRAME
- 60 to 120 minutes (excluding baking time)

Abraxas, the centaur, *was once a warrior, now he is a sage.*
He now knows the things that are learned with age,
how to contain the rage, how to get a pass for backstage.
He is sure that bold dreams must not be caged but bravely engaged.
The centaur knows how painful the truth can be
and he knows how with words to make you feel good.
It is widely acknowledged that no one can rival
his knowledge of the past, of the things that last, of the winds that are fast.
Abraxas also teaches warrior's skills so frightening that they give you the chills,
but he prefers to help build mills and make pills that cure various ills.

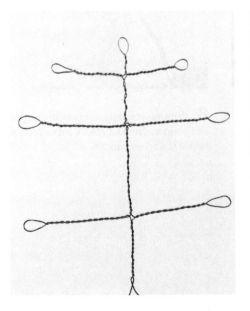

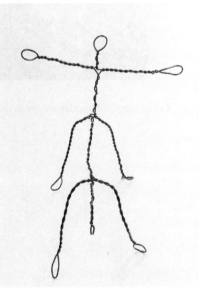

1. Twist some wire to make the centaur's armature as shown. The technique is largely the same as the one used to make the skeleton of the griffins and the unicorns in previous projects

2. Bend the arms and legs as shown, with the human backbone at a right angle to that of the horse.

3. Proceed to make the horse's body up to the stage shown, and bake it. Notice that one of the front legs is raised. To achieve that posture you simply need to bend the wire accordingly before you start covering with clay. Keep in mind, though, that since one leg is now up in the air, the weight of the centaur has to be distributed evenly among his other three legs. To achieve that, put the front leg that is on the ground slightly more to the middle—the hoof should be directly underneath the backbone of the human part. Ideally, the hooves, hind leg, and front supporting leg should form an isosceles triangle.

4. Once you have made sure that the centaur can firmly stand on his legs, proceed to cover the human backbone with foil and a coat of flesh-colored clay.

5. Centaurs are very athletic, so we give Abraxas a six-pack. Roll out six balls and plaster them onto the torso as shown. The lowermost ones are slightly elongated.

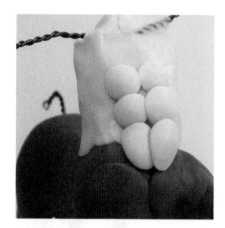

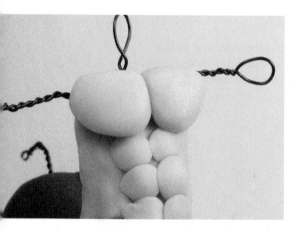

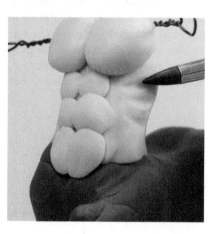

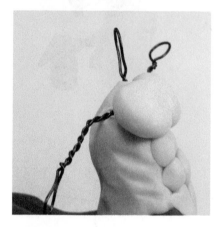

6. Gently smudge the edges of the abdominal muscles into the torso. Roll a set of bigger clay balls, squish them a little, and stick them above the six-pack to make the chest. Almost all the muscles we make here are made out of simple balls of clay, squished to a different degree and attached to one another. Generally, the rounder the balls are, and the more you forget to smudge in the edges into the surrounding clay, the more muscular your critter will be. Flatter and more egglike shapes make for a less buff but still athletic centaur.

7. Use the tip of the clay shaper to draw a few ribs.

8. Bend the armature arms slightly back and down as demonstrated. Centaurs rarely have a scarecrow posture.

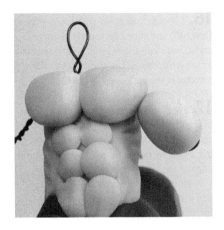

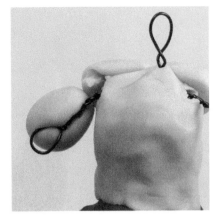

9. To make biceps, roll a ball of clay and stick it on top of the armature and next to the chest as shown. The armature should sink in the muscle as you push from front to back. Tighten the biceps around the upper arm's armature bone.

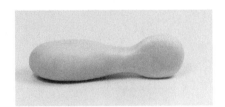

10. The hand of the centaur is made as part of his lower arm. Roll out a short clay baguette, gently squeeze one end and roll it between your index finger and thumb right next to the flat part. The flat extremity will be the palm and the thinner part—the wrist.

11. Attach four snakes with round end to the palm; these should be of relative size and in the formation shown.

12. Turn the hand around; this will be the backside of the hand. Use the clay shaper to eliminate seams and make knuckles. You can close the hand into a fist by bending each finger and the thumb once in their middle and at the knuckles, or arrange them in another formation.

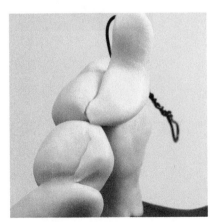

13. With your fingers, stick the lower arm to the biceps at an angle—the armature should reach almost halfway into the elbow joint. Use a clay shaper to smoothen.

14. Add triceps on the back of the biceps; this will cover the scar from the wire that went into the clay.

15. Use a thick squished snake as shown to make what we want to look like the trapezoid and neck muscles.

16. Make a small dome with round edges (half ball) and stick it on top of the arm, chest, and trapezoid muscles as shown. Push as shown to deflate the chest a little and smudge in the upper part of the shoulder.

17. Put a metal bracelet around one wrist of the centaur. The bracelet is made by squishing flat a snake of clay and cutting out a long rectangle from it to get the sharp edge of the bracelet.

Using the handle tip of the clay shaper, add a small shallow dents on the chest for nipples.

18. Now that the centaur has a body, it is time to make a head. Pinch a ball of clay as shown to get the nose protrusion. Make sure to get a lot of clay between your fingers because the character will have a rather large nose.

19. Push straight on the face to define where the nose ends. Use the clay shapers to make the nostrils, from the outside and the inside.

20. Put a small eye socket in the head using the handle tip of the clay shaper. Wrap a ball of glow-in-the-dark polymer clay in a squished clay worm and insert into the eye socket.

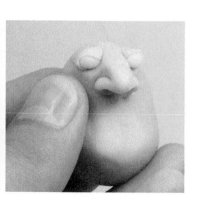

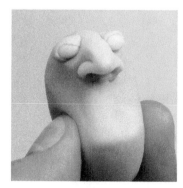

21. Push gently with your thumb to make the cheeks of the centaur flat.

22. Press lightly as shown to make the face narrower. Squeeze under the chin as well.

23. Use a needle to draw a mouth. Make sure to leave a large lower jaw and chin.

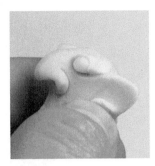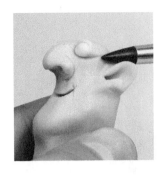

24. Pull an ear out of the centaur's head; delimit it from top and bottom and put a hole in it with the taper-point clay shaper.

25. Add a forehead. Use a clay shaper to cover your tracks.

26. Push with the taper-point clay shaper to make the corners of the mouth.

27. For a lower lip, put a small clay worm horizontally underneath the mouth line and smudge its end in to the jaw.

28. Choose a brown color different that that of the horse's body. Make two short, thick clay snakes and put them on top of the eyelids to make eyebrows. Make the beard by wrapping a sheet of brown clay (obtained by squishing a round-ended snake) around the lower jaw.

29. Give the centaur elegant thin side-burns to connect the hair on his head to his beard.

30. Add hair to the top of the head.

31. Make several streaks of hair by squishing irregularly shaped pieces of clay and arrange them parallel to each other.

32. Here is your centaur's head ready to be put on the centaur's neck.

33. Use a small tube to make a pattern of interlocking circles on the hair, eyebrow, and beard of the creature to create the impression his hair is curly. The technique is similar to the one used for the scales of the mermaid, only this time you can imprint full circles on the clay. Finally, pinch the beard as shown. You may have to repeat some of the circles afterward.

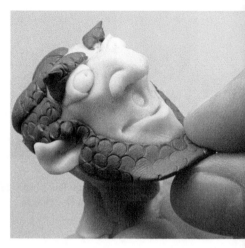

34. Here is the finished front of the centaur. The only thing left to take care of is the back of the centaur.

35. The back of the centaur has a human part and a horse part. For the horse part, cover the armature tail with streaks as you did for the unicorn, and draw some individual hairs on it with the tip of a needle.

36. For the back of the human, we make a cloak out of a flat rectangle of green clay. Squeeze the two upper corners of the rectangle as shown. Gently pull on the bit between your fingers to elongate it, as this is the end that goes around the centaur's neck, which is quite strong.

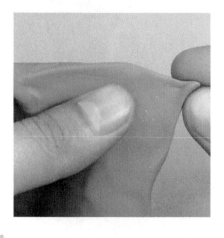

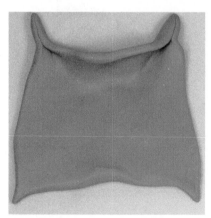

37. Give the lower corners an irregular shape as well; the purpose of this exercise is that, when you put the cloak around the shoulders of the centaur, it will look as if it is floating in the air. If you have a perfect geometric shape, the cloak will look static. Now, because the centaur is half horse, he is more likely to run with the wind rather than sit still. At great speeds, fabric moves.

38. Here is what the cloak looks like after the tweaking in the previous two steps.

39. Wrap the cloak around the neck of the centaur to cover his back.

40. Notice that we changed the color of the hooves by wrapping them with thin sheets of gold clay; that way, the size of the hooves increased a little as well.

variations

The old warrior centaur, wielder of the spear, who taught Achilles and many other ancient heroes.

The wise centaur, the wielder of reason.

chapter 11
THE LEVIATHAN

The Leviathan

The leviathan is a huge sea creature. There were, once upon a time real, now-extinct fish species that frightened sailors, and this fear probably started the myth in ancient times. Sometimes large animals, especially whales, are called leviathans. (You may call leviathan everything of its kind that is unusually large.) Myth has it that the leviathan lives in the sea, takes pride in his scales, has beautiful skin, has fins that are silver, and radiates light. It is rumored that the leviathan has seven lives. He is extremely powerful. He bends iron as straws and brass seems to him like rotten wood. He makes the water boil, has a fiery breath, and sends smoke out of his nostrils. His fierce teeth terribly frighten those who see him.

The leviathan project is one that tests patience more than skill. Patience is the most important tool for making the leviathan.

MATERIALS
- polymer clay in the following colors: orange, white, black, pink, brown, green, beige, violet, silver effect, several different kinds of blue, gold effect
- stiff artist's wire
- baking foil
- scrap clay

TOOLS
- 3 ceramic tiles for work surface
- linemen's pliers
- needle-nose pliers
- wire cutter

TIME FRAME
- over 4 hours (excluding baking time)

The Leviathan has no suntan, *because he lives far from the Sudan.*
He lives deep in the sea where there is no one except him that you can see.
He is the terror of every seaman; he does not have a single fan.
This is what they say about him every now and then.
But this a mistake—these stories are a fake.
The leviathan is a gentleman—he helps boatmen, Dutchmen,
earth men, yachtsmen, ship men, and in general all men
when they roam his sea domain.
Powerful as he is from his good deeds he expects neither gain nor fame.
Still the question came, "For his bad reputation whom are we to blame?"
All excuses are lame. Storytellers must reconsider and tell the true story of the Leviathan's glory.
Then the sailors will not worry when they see the Leviathan's gigantic body.

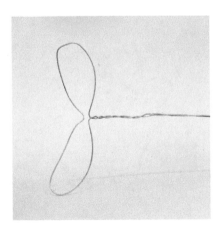

1. Take a 35" (88.9 cm) piece of stiff wire and bend it in two. Curve the end of it so that it looks like a tail fin.

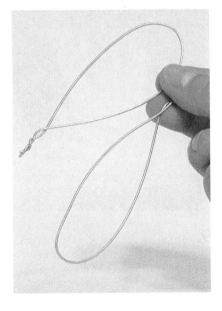

2. Make two identical fins from two 10"(25.4 cm) pieces of wire. Those measurements are just a guideline. They can vary a lot, depending on your own ideas of the size of the fins of the leviathan. The size also depends on the size of your oven. Generally, the size of the oven is the limit of how big a creature can get. A good way to define how big the wire skeleton of the biggest creature must be is the following: when you have the wire skeleton ready, place it in the oven. If there is a distance of 4" (10.2 cm) between the skeleton and the oven walls, this is the biggest skeleton possible. If the distance is smaller, make the skeleton smaller. If the distance is bigger, make a bigger skeleton. Make sure that the fins have a pointed tip, so that later on they can easily be attached to the body.

3. Starting from the tail fin, curve the spine of the leviathan.

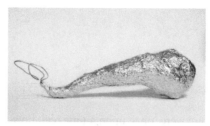

4. Wrap the body with foil. At this point you should be quite accustomed to this technique. The foil stuffing of the body must have a droplet-like shape.

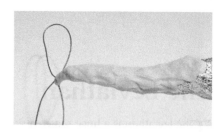

5. Go through your clay supplies. Find all scrap clay, clay that is too soft to use on other projects and start to cover the stuffing. Go slowly and make sure that there are no air bubbles between the foil and the scrap clay cover.

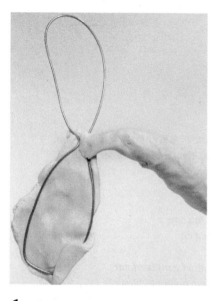

6. If possible make the clay cover of the tail fin thinner than the cover of the body.

7. When the entire body is covered with scrap/soft clay, turn your attention to the head. Add two strips of clay for the leviathan's eyebrows and a strip of clay for the lower lip/jaw.

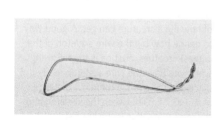

8. Bend the fins as shown.

9. Use the needle-nose pliers to hold the fin and insert its pointy end through the clay cover into the foil core of the leviathan's body.

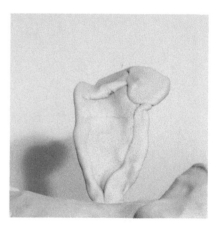

10. Once the fin is attached, cover it with clay. Again, try to make this cover thinner than the clay cover of the body. Do the same for the other fin.

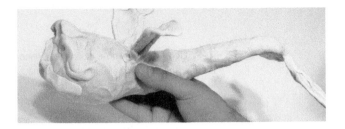

11. This is what the entire body must look like at this point.

12. Cover your baking tray with foil and place the leviathan on it. Make a foil brick to support the head of the creature during the baking. At this point the leviathan must be baked for the first of three times.

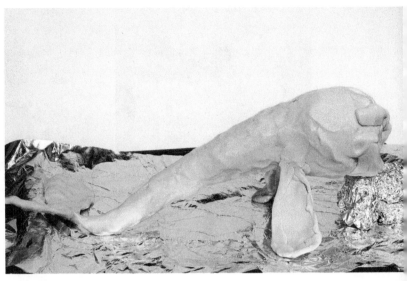

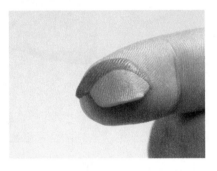

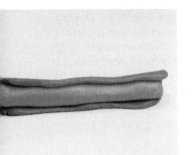

13. Usually with projects that require multiple baking there arises the question what to do during the half hour of baking and the other half hour of cooling. With the leviathan, you can use this time to make the scales. The scales are made using the simplest millefiori technique. Roll a cylinder of clay and make a flat clay strip that is as long as the cylinder. Wrap half of the cylinder with the strip. Cut it in slices. Press the slice between your thumb and index fingers. Here is one of the scales. Make as many scales as possible. Each of the leviathans shown in this chapter required several hundred scales.

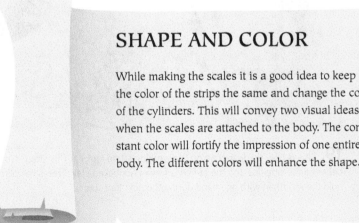

SHAPE AND COLOR

While making the scales it is a good idea to keep the color of the strips the same and change the color of the cylinders. This will convey two visual ideas when the scales are attached to the body. The constant color will fortify the impression of one entire body. The different colors will enhance the shape.

14. Lightly ball up some baking foil. Place it under the leviathan and firmly press the leviathan on it as shown. Now you have a working stand that will enable you to work on all sides of the leviathan's belly and fins. These are demonstrations of the different angles of rotating the work stand.

  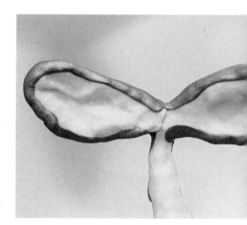

15. Start covering the tail fin with strips of silver or glittering effect color of your choice.

16. First, cover the lower side of the tail fin with strips of clay.

17. The strips that cover the edges must overlap from the lower to the upper side. Since at this point only a small part of the body is covered with nonbaked clay, and the body can be held in hand easily, it is a good idea to cover the upper side of the tail fin with strips, too.

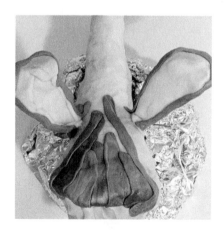 

18. Once the tail fin is covered, turn your attention to the other fins. Cover their edges with a long strip of clay. Cover the "neck" of the leviathan with strips of different shades of silver clay.

19. This is how the leviathan on the working stand looks at this stage. Note that a place between the side fins and the tail fin is free of nonbaked clay. This is the place that you will hold the leviathan with one hand during the next few steps.

Sculpting Mythical Creatures out of Polymer Clay

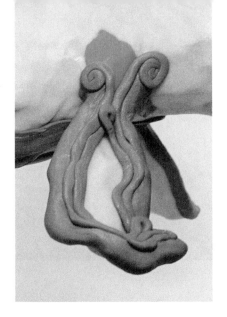

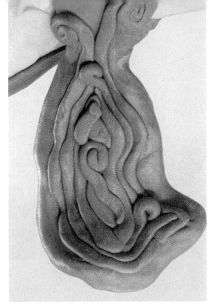

20. Prepare several snakes of silver clay. Curl their ends, and with the rest of the snake, follow the shape of the upper side of the side fin. Cover the entire upper side. Put the curves on arbitrary places.

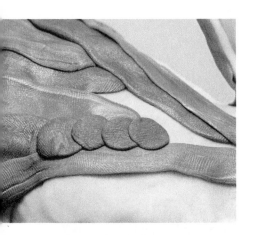

21. Go to the neck of the creature and cover the baked surface with silver disks/scales.

22. Cover the lower side of the side fins with simple silver scales like the red ones of the dragon.

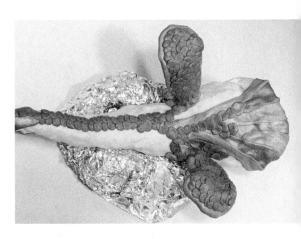

23. Connect the neck and the tail of the creature with a line of silver scales.

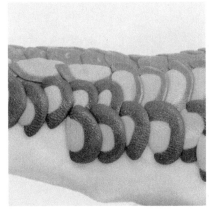

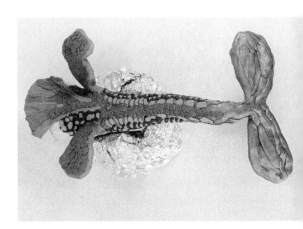

24. On the sides of that connecting line, add some pink scales. Once those are added, bake the creature once again. The belly of the leviathan, the tail fin, and the side fins are covered with scales and shaped. As far as they go they are finished, and after they are baked the creature will stand on its own and it will be possible to work easily on its head and back.

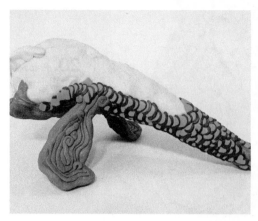

25. With the sea monster standing fine on its own, start to cover its back with blue scales.

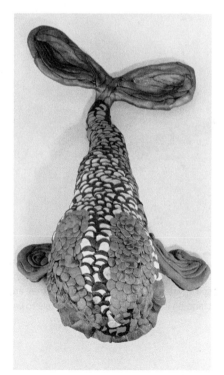

26. The color patterns of scale coverage are absolutely arbitrary and a matter of personal choice. Keep in mind that, like every living creature, a leviathan may have scars, burns, and nonsymmetrical body pigmentation. And since there are no experts in mythical biology, anything you decide is correct.

27. Make two orange balls for the bases of the leviathan's eyeballs. Press those lightly in the middle.

28. Add a big white eyeball. Add a flat gold disk for the iris, a smaller black disk for the pupil, and an even smaller white disk for the light reflection in the pupil.

29. Add a blue lower eyelid.

30. Add a pink upper eyelid and overlap it with another silver eyelid.

31. Make eyebrows of a strong vibrant color of your choice.

32. Attach a thick strip of clay for the lower jaw of the creature.

33. Make the mouth corners. Now there is a choice to be made: Do you prefer your leviathan to have fierce teeth or have no teeth on account of his old age? If you decide to leave him toothless, skip the next two steps.

34. Add big fierce, sharp teeth to the lower jaw.

35. Cover the roots of the teeth with a snake of silver-effect clay.

36. Mix different shades of blue.

37. Make three piles, each of a dozen curled snakes of different blue. Place them on three separate small work surfaces. These are the waves that the Leviathan makes when he swims.

38. Put the three small work surfaces with the wave piles on an upside-down, large baking dish. Gently hold the leviathan by the baked part of the tail and adjust the wave piles so that under each of the side fins and under the tail there is a pile of waves. Bake the monster.

Creation process does not always have a nice step-by-step flow. One can hardly think of everything before starting work. We want to illustrate a consideration that was not made while making the previous leviathan and is made now. The ships are added to illustrate the size of the previous leviathan and are attached directly to the waves under the creature's fins. This makes the creature a bit harder to transport and store, so on the current project, the ship will be separate.

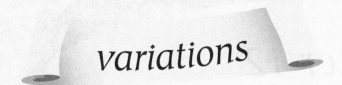

variations

During this baking, it is time to start making an addition to the leviathan project that will show how big and old the creature is in fact. A Viking ship will show perfectly both concepts. The particular thing about Viking ships is the Vikings that stir them. So let's make a Viking.

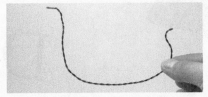

2. Take a piece of wire, bend it in two, and twist it. Curve it as shown to form the middle of the Viking ship.

3. Cover the ship's central beam with brown clay and bake it.

1. Make a ¾" (1.9 cm)-high green T shape. Add on top of it a ¼" (6 mm) diameter flesh-colored ball for the head of the sailor. Make an orange crescent for the beard. Put a gold disk on top of the head for the helmet and add a flesh-colored droplet for the nose. Add two small white balls for the eyes. Attach two small pointy horns to the helmet. Here is the first Viking sailor. Seven of those are needed. By the time you are finished with the first one, the leviathan will be baked and out of the oven.

4. While the central beam of the ship is baking, make a hull.

5. Assign the Vikings to their posts.

6. Put two pieces of unbaked clay on a work surface and attach the central beam of the ship to them as shown. This is your dry dock. Stick the hull with the Vikings to the central beam of the ship.

7. Attach some more beams to finish the ship's hull. Do the same for the other side of the hull.

Make a pile of waves like the ones that were put under the leviathan's fins. Detach the ship from her "dock" and place her on top of the waves.

8. Add two balls of brown clay to the front of the ship and poke two holes in them to make the ship's eyes. Make several silver disks with a gold ball attached in the middle to represent the warriors' shields and attach those to both sides of the ship. Bake her and the crew. Now you have a ship that will witness the greatness of your leviathan and spread the word that he is a good-natured old fellow.

The great battle of the Leviathans took them to a small creek as they were chasing ships full of brave Viking warriors on their way to defeat the dragon from the next project.

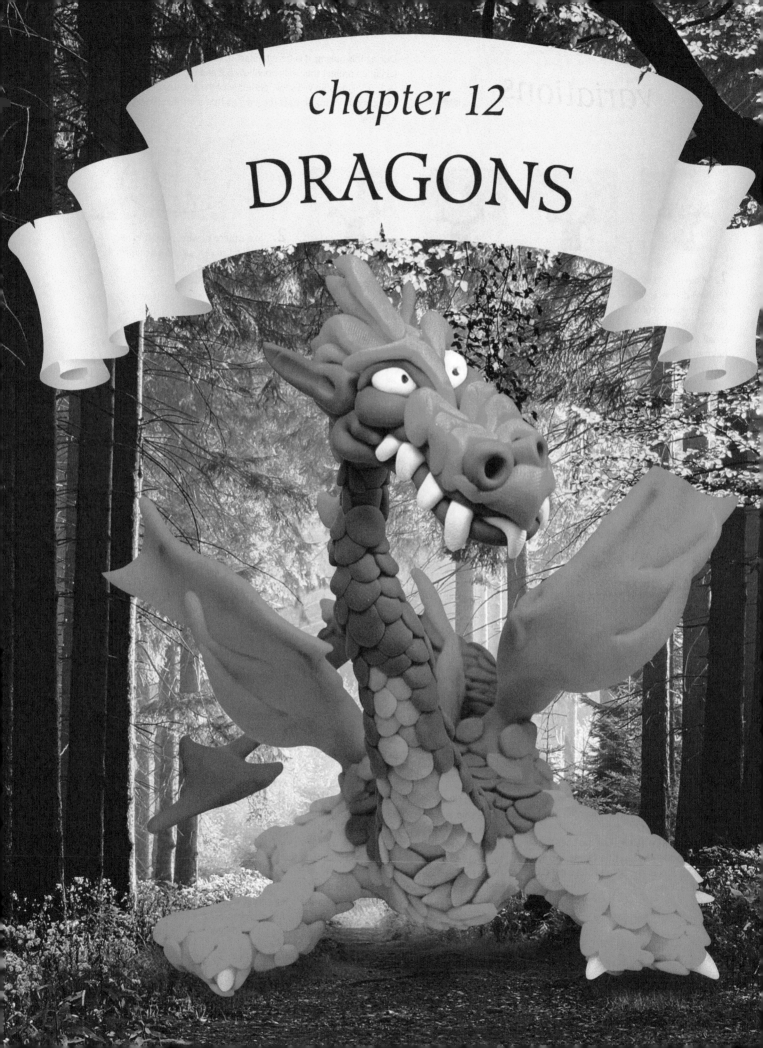

chapter 12
DRAGONS

Xing-fu Babur, the Dragon

Dragons are magical creatures that come in all sizes, shapes, and colors. In most cultures dragons are represented as a mixture of a reptile, a bird, and a horse. It is a common belief that they exhale acid or fire. They have batlike wings and hatch from eggs. These creatures are usually covered with scales and have dorsal spikes. Dragons may have a different number of legs—no legs at all, two legs, four legs, or even more. There are also different theories on the number of heads a dragon has, ranging from one to twelve. In some cultures, dragons are considered to be benevolent creatures and in others they are monsters. Dragons are symbols of both good and bad, depending on the cultural tradition.

For the purposes of this project, the dragon will have one head, four legs, and two wings.

MATERIALS
- polymer clay in the following colors: black, white, different shades of red
- baking foil
- scrap clay
- stiff artist's wire

TOOLS
- linemen's pliers
- needle-nose pliers
- ceramic tile for work surface
- needle
- taper-point clay shaper

TIME FRAME
- 8 hours (excluding baking time)

What is in a dragon? *Firstly magic—a whole wagon!*
Then some history and a pinch of mystery.
Some aeronautics, defiance of all logic.
There are also a lot of scales, rather longish nails,
of the dragons deeds some fairy tales.
Some goodwill that always prevails
and a very sharp tail.
Also in his stomach you must build a strange chemical factory,
so that the flames he exhales would be satisfactory.
Mix all well, add water from a charmed well.
Then bake the creature in a wizard's oven.
When the dragon is ready and cooked
you can let him in the air to goof off.

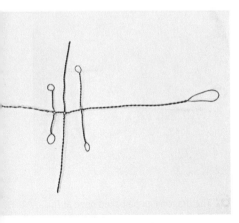

1. Make a skeleton like the one of the griffin. The only difference here is that the prospective neck of the creature must be a lot longer than the one made for the griffin.

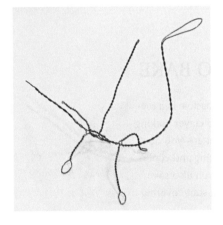

2. Turn the wings and the neck upward from the spine. Bend the legs downward.

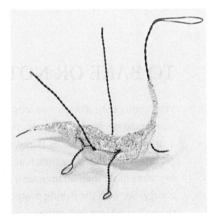

3. Wrap the skeleton in foil.

  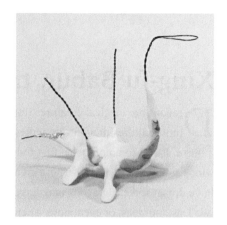

4. Cover everything with soft or scrap clay that wouldn't be used on other projects. Note that a small portion of the tail must stay uncovered.

 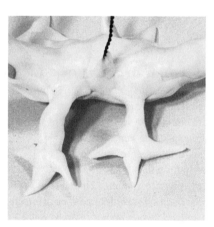 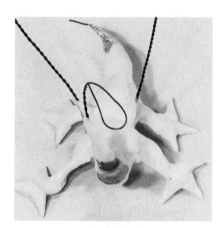

5. Add three pointy droplets to each of the dragon's legs. These droplets are simultaneously the toes and claws of the dragon.

TO BAKE OR NOT TO BAKE

Postponing the baking for as long as possible is a recommendation for the more experienced clayer. Baking a smaller number of times is always better—you don't get distracted, you save time (each baking and cooling takes more than 30 minutes), and you also save energy. So, with the baking postponed, start covering the belly and legs with scales.

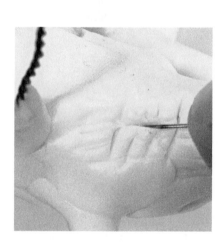

6. The dragon can be baked once at this point. This baking will ensure a solid base that will be easy to hold and work on. If your decision is to bake at this point, be sure to scratch the clay with a needle. This will provide an uneven surface to which the scales will cling better.

TONS OF SCALES

If you work together with a fellow clayer, a classmate, a parent, or anyone else interested in your work, you can ask them to help you make the small balls for the scales—you need a lot of these! This will speed up your work dramatically.

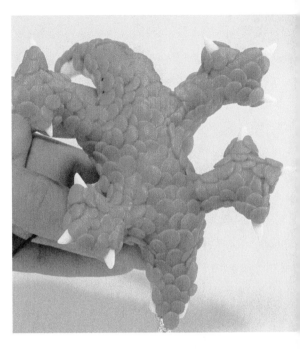

7. It is a good idea to have a number of small red balls ready made. Press the ball between thumb and index finger to create a scale; attach it to the dragon's body.

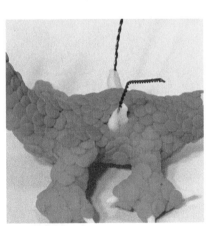

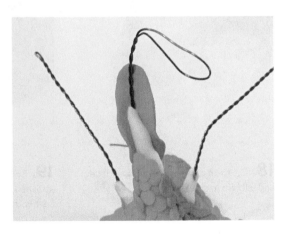

8. Don't forget to leave the pointy tips of the dragon's fingers uncovered—these are his claws.

9. After the feet and the belly are covered with scales, place the dragon on the work surface. Cover his back with scales of a red color different than the one used for the belly and the feet. Bake the creature. Allow it to cool down before you continue.

10. Now part of the dragon is baked and easy to hold. Cover the neck with red clay.

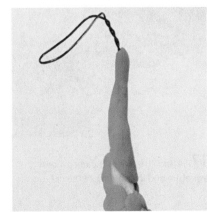

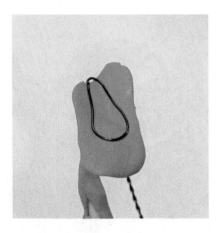

11. Cover the head with red clay.

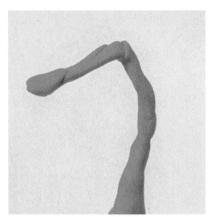

12. Put scales all around the neck of the dragon and on the lower part of the head.

13. Make a thick cylinder of red clay. Hold it three-quarters the way from one end between your thumb and index finger; squeeze. Roll the cylinder at the place you squeezed. Now there is a little ball at one end of the cylinder.

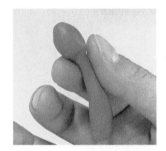

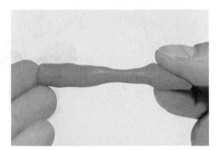

14. Squeeze the ball to flatten it.

15. Hold it from one side and squeeze again to make a pointy end. Do the same to the other side.

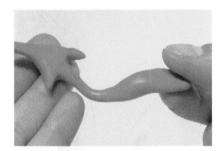

16. This is what the dragon's tail should look like. Carefully hold the tail and with your right hand flatten its other end.

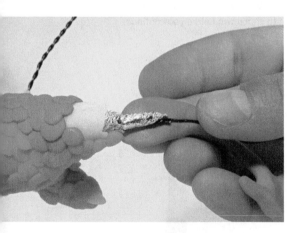

17. Attach the tail to the uncovered armature and foil stuffing of the dragon.

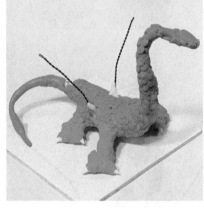

18. Put the dragon on the work surface and tell him to stay put.

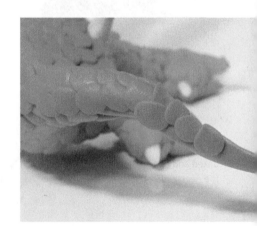

19. Cover the place where the tail was attached to the body with scales, to ensure a smooth transition from the scaled part of the body to the bare tale.

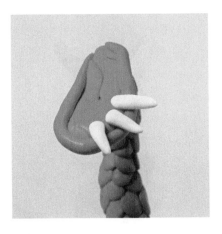

20. Turn your attention to the head of the dragon. Add a lower lip and teeth as shown.

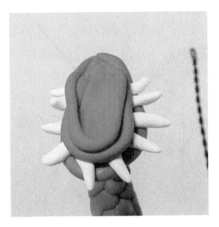

21. Cover the teeth with two upper lips.

22. Make two red cones for the nostrils of the dragon.

23. Don't forget to make the lower eyelids.

24. Make the mouth corners on both sides of the mouth. Add a small ball of red to the back end of the head to add volume to the dragon's skull.

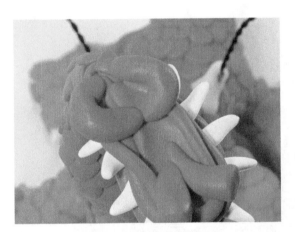

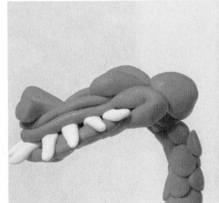

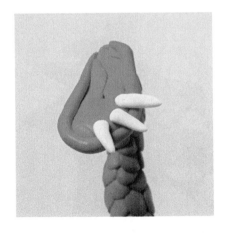

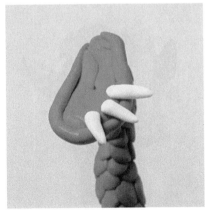

25. Add white eyeballs and the upper eyelids. Be sure to wash your hands before using the white clay. (Remember the Mischievous Colors tip in the Gnome project? See page 15.)

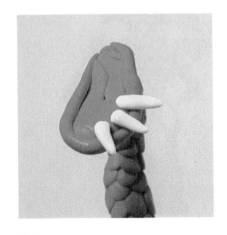

26. Use the taper-point clay shaper to drill the dragon's nostrils.

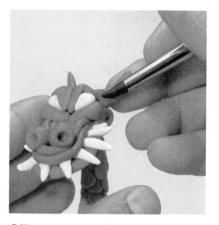 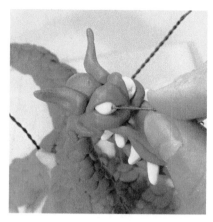 

27. Use the taper-point clay shaper to add the ears of the dragon and curve them.

28. Poke two holes into the eyeballs for the pupils of the dragon's eyes.

29. Make eyebrows.

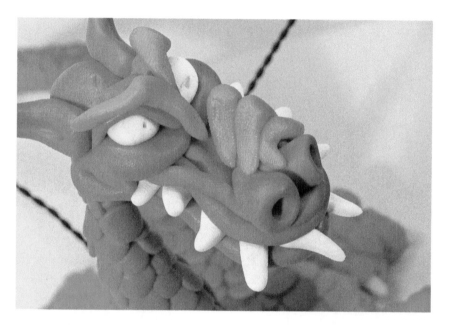

30. Cover the head from the nostrils to the lower eyelids with small clay wrinkles.

31. Push the dragon's teeth downward and add a piece of clay in front of the nostrils to make a pointy upper lip.

32. Cover the dragon's skull with thick pieces of hair.

33. The three upper pieces of hair must be the thickest of all because they form the first and the biggest of the dragon's dorsal spikes.

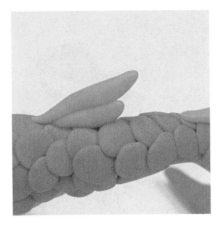

34. Continue making the dorsal spines on the neck, back, and tail of the dragon. The dorsal spines closer to the head may include three pieces and the dorsal spines close to the tail can be made of just two pieces of clay.

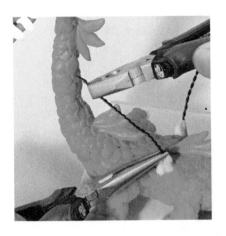

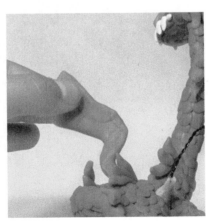

35. Take the needle-nose pliers and hold the armature of the wing at the point where its clay cover ends. Hold the end of the armature with the linemen's pliers and bend the armature toward the head. Holding the armature with the needle-nose pliers is important because it prevents your breaking the baked clay that covers the base of the wing.

36. Bend the wing backward in the middle. No holding with pliers is necessary at this step. These images show the profile of the wing armature and how it should look enface.

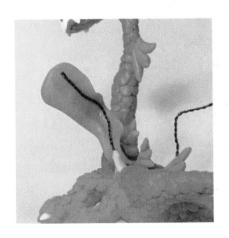

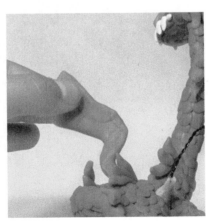

37. Cover the wing armature with clay. Make the wing as thin as possible.

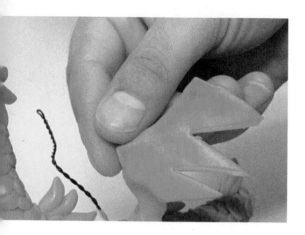

38. Cut the shape of the wing with a pair of scissors.

39. Smooth the surface of the wing, and make the joints and the tips of the wing pointed. Push the pointy edges of the wing upward to overlap with one another.

40. Add more scales to the places where the wings connect to the body. The same thing was done for the tail. Use a clay shaper for the spots that are hard to reach.

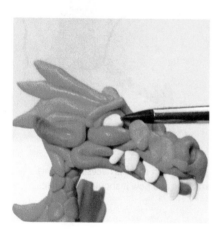

41. Make a really small black ball for the pupil of the dragon's eye. Pick it up with the taper-point clay shaper and install it into the dragon's eye. Do the same for the other eye. Bake the dragon to breathe life into him. Watch out—he might breathe fire!

The majestic fire-breathing Xing-fu Babur is the most powerful and wise of the many varieties of dragons out there.

Sculpting Mythical Creatures out of Polymer Clay

variations

The Fire-Breathing Variety is a must-have for every household in the cold countries of the north.

The Garden Variety eats his greens without much hassle.

The Fancy Chinese Variety brings good luck; nobody knows where he gets it.

The dragon hunter, of gnome descent, has one of the most dangerous jobs in the mythical worlds.

RESOURCES

The Internet

www.dekar-m.com
The finest suppliers of polymer clay in Bulgaria

www.eaudrey.com/myth/
Dave's Mythical Creatures and Places—a great resource on the various species of mythical beings

www.eberhardfaber.de
Manufacturers of the famous Fimo polymer clay

www.glassattic.com
The place where any question about polymer clay will be answered

www.loggia.com/myth/
A resource on mythology

www.mythcritters.com
Variations and tips on making mythical and other imaginary characters

www.pcpolyzine.com
Online polymer clay magazine

www.polymerclaycentral.com
The best polymer clay place on the Net

www.polymerclaydaily.com
A blog written by Cynthia Tinapple of Worthington, which covers almost anything about polymer clay.

www.sculpey.com
One of the finest manufacturers of polymer clay

www.theclaystore.com
One of the best places to shop for polymer clay and tools online

Books

Big Book of Dragons, Monsters, and Other Mythical Creatures (Dover Pictorial Archive Series)
Ernst and Johanna Lehner
(Dover Publications 2004)
ISBN-10: 0486435121
ISBN-13: 978-0486435121

Classical Mythology
Geddes & Grosset
(Geddes & Grosset 2003)
ISBN-10: 1855343487
ISBN-13: 978-1855343481

Dragons: A Natural History
Karl P. N. Shuke
(Simon & Schuster 1995)
ISBN-10: 0684814439
ISBN-13: 978-0684814438

Dragons and Wizards (CD-ROM and Book)
Marty Noble & Eric Gottesman
(Dover Publications 2003)
ISBN-10: 0486995593
ISBN-13: 978-0486995595

How to Draw Animals
Jack Hamm
(Perigee Trade 1983)
ISBN-10: 0399508023
ISBN-13: 978-0399508028

Mythological and Fantastic Creatures CD-ROM and Book
(Dover Publications 2002)
ISBN-10: 0486995100
ISBN-13: 978-0486995106

Mythology Pictures / Mythologische Bilder / Motifs Mythologiques
Pepin Van Roojen
(Pepin Press 2007)
ISBN-10: 9057680661
ISBN-13: 978-9057680663

ABOUT THE AUTHORS

Boris Tilov has been working with polymer clay since his early teenage years. He has lived and studied in his native Bulgaria and the United States. Boris is currently working for a telecommunications company. He maintains a blog, www.claywizard.blogspot.com, dedicated to making chess sets from polymer clay blog and has recently started a "Polymer clay in Bulgaria" group on Facebook.

Boris and Dinko run www.mythcritters.com, where you can find even more variations and tips on making mythical and other imaginary characters.

Dinko Tilov has been sculpting with clay for more than a decade. He is the author of *Creating Fantasy Polymer Characters* (Quarry Books 2004) and runs www.funclay.com, where you can see tons of them. He has lived and studied in Bulgaria, the United States, and France, where he researched the fascinating topic of gargoyles, among other things. Dinko now lives in Sofia, Bulgaria.

Dinko and Boris Tilov

ACKNOWLEDGMENTS

Dinko

I would like to thank Sophia, the fairiest of them all, for her encouragement and support and for helping deal with the growing crowd of mythical beasts.

Thanks to my brother Boris for the good times in this project.

Thank you to the Rockport Publishers' team, for believing in us and our imaginary creations.

Thanks to the inventors of polymer clay and computers.

Boris

Thanks to my wife, Maria, and my daughter, Irina, without whose love and patience none of my clay adventure would have been possible.

Thanks to my brother Dinko for the fun we had writing this book.

Thanks to Rockport Publishers for undertaking the magical journey to create this book.

CPSIA information can be obtained at www.ICGtesting.com
Printed in the USA
LVOW02s2003130614

389951LV00003B/5/P